10 WAYS
TO MAKE YOUR
BUSINESS FAIL

Copyright © 2024 by Tyler Jeffs

Published by Four Rivers Media

All rights reserved. No portion of this book may be reproduced, stored in a retrieval system, or transmitted in any form or by any means—electronic, mechanical, photocopy, recording, scanning, or other—except for brief quotations in critical reviews or articles, without prior written permission of the author.

For foreign and subsidiary rights, contact the author.

Cover design by Sara Young
Cover photo by Andrew van Tilborgh

ISBN:978-1-962401-74-6   1 2 3 4 5 6 7 8 9 10

Printed in the United States of America

Author's note: In many of the stories, the names and details have been changed to protect anonymity . . . and retain as many friends as possible!

TYLER L. JEFFS

10 WAYS
TO MAKE YOUR
BUSINESS FAIL

YOU CAN'T AVOID MISTAKES,
SO LEARN FROM THEM

DEDICATION

I'm deeply grateful to my wife Tiffany for her unwavering support even when she's uncertain, my parents for teaching me a work ethic, my children for teaching what life and love is really all about, and lastly to Almighty God from whom all blessings are realized.

CONTENTS

Introduction 9

CHAPTER 1. **"MY CUSTOMERS SUCK!"** 19

CHAPTER 2. **"MY EMPLOYEES STINK!"** 31

CHAPTER 3. **"IF I WANT IT DONE RIGHT..."** 53

CHAPTER 4. **"CONTINUING ED. IS FOR SUCKERS."** 67

CHAPTER 5. **"HE'S MINE!"** 87

CHAPTER 6. **"THAT CAN WAIT 'TIL TOMORROW."** 103

CHAPTER 7. **"IT WAS JUST A LITTLE LIE."** 115

CHAPTER 8. **"I CAN'T AFFORD IT."** 129

CHAPTER 9. **"IT'S ALL ABOUT ME."** 145

CHAPTER 10. **"IF ONLY..."** 159

Endnotes 173

INTRODUCTION

Winners are not afraid of losing. But losers are.
If you avoid failure, you also avoid success.
—Robert Kiyosaki

It was right at the top of my bucket list. I'd seen plenty of videos of people jumping out of planes, screaming in free fall, and then having the time of their lives when the parachute opened, and they were dots in the big blue sky. It looked like fun. I just had to do it at least once for bragging rights.

My wife Tiffany and I found a skydiving service that looked reputable. (At least they didn't list any deaths on their website.) We reserved our time slot, and I put it out of my mind. I knew that if I thought about it too much, I'd throw up. A couple of weeks later, we found ourselves suited up and getting the safety check before we boarded the plane. The tuna can they called a plane climbed beyond what seemed impossibly high. I'd like to say I was having second thoughts, but I was way beyond that. The pilot told us our present altitude was only a third of the way up, and this was our last time to back out. I wanted to yell, "Get me down!" I wasn't thinking about wasting the money I'd paid; I was planning to pay double to land as soon as possible. But Tiffany patted me on the leg, smiled, and yelled through the noise, "Everything will be fine! Just relax and enjoy the ride!"

The jump instructor must have never taken a class on reading body language. He acted like this jump was going to be the highlight of his life. He gave me a thumbs up and, above the noise of the engine, yelled, "Stick your legs out the door!" I couldn't do it. It took all my strength in my arms to lift my legs out the door because my legs knew better than to jump out of that plane! To encourage me, he grinned and yelled, "Take a deep breath and take in the view." It was a trick. While I was taking a deep breath, he connected his harness to mine and pushed us out the door!

Instantly, I was in a full-blown panic. I thought I might throw up, and at 120 miles an hour, it wasn't going to be pretty. I tried to repeat all the things I'd said since we signed up for the trip: "This is going to be so much fun!" "We'll never forget the experience!" "Why haven't we done this before?" But my positive affirmations didn't make a dent in the hard fact that I was hurtling toward *terra firma* with a strange dude strapped to my back.

After what seemed like hours, he pulled the rip cord. Huh... that's odd. I was expecting a big jolt when the chute opened, but it was more like a little bump. The chute hadn't opened. Now the instructor panicked!

I was sure I was soiling my underwear (and everything else I had on), but I realized it didn't matter because when I hit the ground at this speed... you get the idea. I hoped the guy had a good backup plan, preferably one that didn't involve impending death. It's odd what goes through your mind when your adrenaline level redlines. I remembered the joke, "What's the last thing that goes through a bug's mind when he hits the windshield? His butt!" Somehow, the joke wasn't as funny as I remembered it.

After he pulled the rip cord, we hurtled toward the ground for about thirty seconds. (That's what he told me later, but it had to be much longer than that.) I heard a "ping." It was the quick release on the main chute. Now, it was unattached above us. My eyes surveyed the ground directly under us. As I rolled over my right shoulder, I looked to see exactly where I would die when we hit. Would we land in the ocean? On a silo? On a road? I hoped for the ocean, but I didn't have a vote. Ten seconds later, he pulled the rip cord on the emergency chute. When it opened, it jerked us almost to a cold stop. I screamed, "Get me to the ground, Robbie! Please, don't do any extras. Just get my behind where it belongs—on dry ground!"

The next couple of minutes of floating through the air should have been the fun part, but I'm not sure "fun" correlates with five gallons of adrenaline coursing through my body. As we got closer to the ground, the overload of brain chemicals began to return to normal. We finally touched Mother Earth, but we lay in the grass for a long time, trying to breathe again.

And Tiffany? She and her instructor jumped a few seconds after us. When he saw what was happening to us, he steered them away so she couldn't watch the carnage. When she landed, she was so excited. It was, she exclaimed, the most fun she'd had in years. She had done barrel rolls and all kinds of neat tricks with her jump instructor.

He told her to go over to check on me. When she came to us, she shook her head and asked, "What are you two doing? Get up. Let's compare our jumps!"

Compare? Really? I let her tell her story first, partly because I didn't want to ruin her enthusiasm and because I was still on the backside of hyperventilating. When she finished with her account of the glory of drifting through space, I said, "That's great. Mine was just as memorable... but not for the same reasons."

When we got back to the hangar, the plane had landed, and all the employees came out to be sure I was okay (and to see if I was going to sue them). Before we went up, I had watched the instructional video online and again in the hangar, but I didn't recall the part about a parachute not opening or how to wash underwear after that happens. I've seen many a shirt that says something like this: "I visited this place or that place, and all I got was this lousy T-shirt." Well, I gotta tell ya, I didn't even get the T-shirt!!

I'll always remember Robbie Young at Skydive Maui in Hana for his calmness and professionalism in such an extraordinary and terrifying drama. This experience is a metaphor for anyone who is doing something he's never done before: it's absolutely critical to be tied to the right people from the beginning. Hanging your shingle out with your name on it is as terrifying and thrilling as skydiving the first time. You tie your success to someone else—a partner, a banker, or a parent company. Your hopes and fears are both sky-high.

You have big dreams, but pretty quickly, you realize you don't know jack about what you're doing. In the air, my life was determined by a guy I'd just met and didn't know at all. In starting a business, your finances, your future, and your reputation are determined by people you hope will come through when you need them. Sure, you've told your spouse about your dreams and plans. You can talk about them a lot, but your spouse can't know the depths of your dreams and dreads without carrying the weight of the responsibility for success.

There were actually three of us who went to Skydive Maui that day. A friend stayed on the ground to video our descent. Not long after Robbie and I left the plane, my friend realized he might be capturing the dramatic moments before, during, and after my death. He could see us spiraling out of control, and he was worried, but he had no idea of the hell of those few minutes. No matter how supportive your spouse and friends are, you still feel you're abandoned on a deserted island—or hurtling through space with a maniac strapped to your back. Many of those around you will see how you're putting your vision into practice, but they won't (and can't) fully appreciate your struggles, no matter how intense they may be.

This book is for people who are planning to start a business. You'll read about enough failures and stupid mistakes to make you think twice . . . and if you decide to go ahead, you'll have a better idea of what's coming.

This book is for people who have started a business and are barely treading water (or drowning!) in the first year or so. You'll be able to identify what went wrong and take bold steps to correct your mistakes.

This book is for professional coaches to use with their clients. You can use my errors as teaching points about what not to do.

This book is for family members and friends who love entrepreneurs. You'll gain a better understanding of the pressure the person is under, where the stress points are, and how you can help—or maybe just get out of the way!

This book is even for politicians who need to understand small business owners, so they can more wisely allocate the sacred funds of taxpayers.

Whoever you are, I'm giving you an invitation and a warning. I want to invite you to be brutally honest about the ways you flirt with ten common mistakes that can kill a career, and I warn you that a lack of honesty will eventually crush you. How do I know?

If you are not in the process of becoming the person you want to be, you are automatically engaged in becoming the person you don't want to be. —Dale Carnegie

---

If you want to be the very best in real estate, learn from Robert Kiyosaki. If you want leadership development skills, go to Tony Robbins. If you need to overcome adversity, check out Nick Vujicic. If you need a motivational shot in the arm, listen to Denzel Washington's speeches. But if you want sharp insights about failure, learn from the best . . . learn from me. The other leaders have amazing talents and experiences. They've conquered Mt. Everest in their fields, carving their names in the sacred halls of honor. They can inspire you, but they may not walk with you through the muck and mire of failure where you learn life's most valuable lessons. I've been there more times than I can count. Come with me. When you read this, please, please be introspective and ask yourself,

"Is this me?"

"Could it possibly be?"

"Do I do that?"

"Am I too afraid to try something great?"

"Am I too impulsive?"

"Who is brave enough to tell me the truth about myself?"

Have I become a me monster?

Has greed spoiled me?

Have I ruined relationships to further my own goals?

In my years starting and growing a business, I've known many gifted people who have made it, but I've also known very smart and talented people who didn't get where they wanted to go. They mentally allowed the pressure to eat them alive and ran themselves out of business. My heart goes out to every person who has a dream like mine. Along the way, I've made more than my fair share of blunders. Some have cost me a lot of money; others have cost something far more valuable: relationships. I don't want you to make my mistakes, or if you do, I want you to learn from them more quickly and thoroughly than I did.

I've screwed up enough to be considered an expert in failure. You can go to Tony Robbins and other incredible leaders to learn how to succeed, but if you want a master class on failure, I'm your guy.

That's my talent. That's my gift. That's my contribution to men and women in business.

Every author gives an implicit, if not explicit, promise. My promise is that if you'll be ruthlessly honest as you read these chapters, your sense of purpose will be clarified, your passion will be directed, your relationships at work and home will be richer, you'll make more money, you'll have more friends, you'll be seen as an asset in your community, and you'll sleep better at night because your conscience will be clear. You'll receive plenty of benefits, and you'll pay them forward into the lives of many others. How's that?

Failure is a terrific teacher. Pay attention. You'll need the lessons it teaches.

Remember: the only thing standing between you and your dreams is what you can learn from your failures, dumb mistakes, lack of talent, and less-than-sterling personality.

My goal isn't to put you down or be self-deprecating. It's just to remind each of us that we weren't born all-stars, but we don't have to settle for being mediocre. To be great requires clear-eyed honesty about what leads to failure. I have had business owners read this and directly ask me, "Were you talking about me?" The answer is yes, I'm talking about you, and I hope you recognize that. Every business owner will find a version of themselves in every chapter and if you're open enough to become vulnerable to that knowledge, you will be better off once you take action. Your response to failure defines you. Don't screw it up!

YOU CAN'T
AVOID MISTAKES,
SO LEARN FROM THEM

Don't customers know they exist for your success, and they should be grateful you're even willing to pay attention to them? Can't they see you're building a business to become rich, and they need to work around your schedule and be more considerate of you? Why do they have to be such a massive pain in the butt anyway? What a bunch of whiners! Why all the questions already? Just let me swipe your card and move on!

CHAPTER 1
"MY CUSTOMERS SUCK!"

Customer service shouldn't just be a department, it should be the entire company.
—Tony Hsieh

Sometimes, yes, customers suck, but every business—and I mean every business—is in the service industry. If we don't serve customers well, our doors won't stay open very long.

Actually, customers don't get enough credit for what they do for your company. They are your lifeblood. Your business only exists because they are paying you for goods and services! Instead of complaining about the few who are a genuine pain in the butt, why not honor them for what they do for you?

Maybe it's just me, but I don't think so. Not long ago, I wanted to switch my cellular carrier. I researched plans the leading companies offered, weighed the options, and made a decision. As a courtesy, I called my existing company to tell them I was going to switch and close the billing cycle. A lady answered my call and introduced herself as Nancy (and she sounded like she lived down the street, not on the other side of the world). She was very polite and gracious.

She thanked me for trusting her company during the time I was a customer, and she said, "If you ever want to come back, we'll be glad to have you." Since I was taking business away from her carrier, she could have been snarky. She wasn't at all.

Then I called the new company. I expected nothing less than how Nancy had treated me, but that's not exactly what happened. I'm not the sharpest linguist in the neighborhood, but I could tell this guy "isn't from around here." I'm sure he had been trained to be pleasant and efficient. He was neither. I described the plan I wanted, and I could hear his disgust. "We don't carry that anymore."

"It's on your website," I explained.

"It shouldn't be," he snapped.

"Well, I can't help that. Do you have something similar?"

"You'll have to look at the website."

"Uh, I just did. That's what I'm telling you."

"Maybe you looked at the wrong one."

That did it. I hung up and called Nancy back to reenlist my old plan. Why? Because she didn't treat me like my call ruined her day.

What's the problem? It's seeing customers (me, in this instance) as annoyances—even adversaries. Do you think they notice? Absolutely. How many times have you heard people talk about customer service (of an insurance company, cable provider, plumber, and every other type of company under the sun), and sneer, "I hate them! I wish I'd never done business with them!" We've all done it. I wonder how many of your clients have said that about you!

Sometimes, the problem is with the primary contact person who handles sales and customer service. This person may be having a bad day, but if it becomes a bad week, a bad month, or a bad quarter, it's a real problem for the business. I'm a huge believer that when you're in any type of customer service, you should be talking to people with flavored sugar dripping off your lips.

> *You are serving a customer, not a life sentence.*
> *Learn how to enjoy your work.*—Laurie McIntosh

Or the problem may be systemic, coming from the top. Some business owners and managers value hitting quotas at all costs, which means they don't give a rip about how their salespeople get there. They pressure, they threaten, they manipulate, they compare, and they use every trick in the book to put the heat on those who relate to customers. When a customer has a problem, the decision matrix is only about getting as much money from her as possible. The maxim, "The customer is always right," goes out the window. Some companies make substitutions, returns, exceptions, and any grace to the customer virtually impossible for those in sales. In fact, many of those companies make it almost impossible for a complaint to even be lodged in the first place. (Their websites look beautiful, but they're a maze with a thousand dead ends.)

One of the biggest failures in business is treating customers as adversaries instead of being their foremost advocates. You wouldn't be in business without them, and you can't stay in business if your people aren't trained, resourced, and rewarded for making customers satisfied . . . if not ecstatic!

Salespeople are there to serve, not demand or condemn.

I've talked with people in sales who acted like the consumer was obligated to buy from them, and they were offended if they didn't. In some of my interactions with salespeople, they were obviously upset with me, not just when I said "no," but when I asked questions. That's turning the seller-buyer relationship upside down! It's totally wrong for those in sales to be judgmental of potential buyers for making their purchasing decisions. It's entirely their choice. Salespeople are there to serve, not demand or condemn. My request to you is this: Be different... on purpose.

Research by Microsoft found that "90% of consumers believe customer service is somewhat to very important in the choice of a brand," and "58% of consumers choose to switch companies because of poor customer service experience."[1] Another study found that customer experience is more important than price and product. As they walk out the proverbial door because of a bad experience, 54% of customers insist on speaking to someone up the chain of command in the company, and 52% complain to family and friends about their experience with the company.[2]

It doesn't take a million-dollar research program to identify the most common customer service complaints: feeling ignored, getting the runaround, lack of knowledge about products, overpromising, rudeness, and when customers can easily tell the CSR is from a country in South Asia, but he says, "My name is Bob." I hate to say it, but I'm in that boat. When I call customer service and hear an automated system or a foreigner with broken English, I expect it to be a rotten experience. Instantly, I feel disgusted because this is a battle I don't want to fight.

Certainly, investments in training team members and flexibility in working with customers cost the company, but good customer service pays huge dividends, including:

- Corporate pride—Employees want to work for a company that treats customers with integrity and respect.
- Retention of great employees—Poor customer service drives customers away and also drives your best employees to other companies where they're treated well.
- Repeat customers—Satisfied consumers tend to stay with you instead of jumping to find an alternative.
- Viral marketing—Happy customers, maybe online but certainly in person, are eager to tell others about your excellent service.
- Higher profits—As I mentioned, when your customers are happy, they'll stay with you. Your new customers don't replace the ones who left; they add to the bottom line. And when your employees are happy, you don't spend as much time and money on hiring and training new staff members.

But customer perceptions aren't static. They change depending on how they're treated. The *Journal of Marketing* published a study of "Transformational Relationship Events" in the lives of almost nine thousand people. They found that "the impact of a customer complaint about a relational issue (i.e., how they were treated) had a more negative impact on retention" than a complaint about a product.

"When a customer already has a good relationship, a relational issue is more threatening to long-term loyalty because it causes the customer to reassess the nature of their relationship ('I wonder if they deserve my loyalty.')." A study by the same team of researchers found:

> Early in a relationship, gestures to exceed relational expectations can have a huge positive impact on customer loyalty. And this is a good thing because it not only benefits the bottom line, but it also buffers the company against the negative impact of the occasional product or service failure. However, the deepening of the relationship with the customer also makes the company more susceptible to falling off a cliff as relational expectations rise and failure to meet expectations causes even greater damage.

They conclude:

> Because of this, companies must take extra care to deliver relationally to their most loyal customers. They must ensure that these customers are treated well interpersonally, that promises are kept, and that customer interests are made a priority in individual interactions. And, fortunately, when a relational failure does occur, the research also found in a subsequent study that proactive communication (e.g., speaking on a regular basis) and a genuine apology dampened some of the negative impact of a relational failure with the company's most loyal customers.[3]

If you're starting a business, you're in charge of sales, or you're a new hire as a CSR, you're under enormous stress to produce, but use the energy inherent in that stress to build bonds of trust with consumers. It makes a huge difference.

Courteous treatment will make a customer a walking advertisement.—J. C. Penney

---

All the training in the world can't take the place of simple acts of kindness. A friend, I'll call him Wade, lives on the Gulf Coast near the Texas-Louisiana border. A few years ago, when a Category 5 hurricane barreled toward his home, he and a friend helped each other board their windows while their wives and kids headed north out of the storm's path. Wade and his friend finished putting plywood over their windows, went to bed utterly exhausted, and left the next morning just hours before the projected landfall. They heard on the news about more than a million people clogging the roads north of their city, so in the dawn light with the winds already blowing at gale strength, they headed west to beat the traffic. They thought they'd beaten the system . . . until the Texas State Troopers, who turned all the traffic north into the quagmire of traffic, stopped them at a crossroads. After a couple of hours and moving only a mile or so, Wade's car began to overheat. The temperature gauge redlined, so he stopped to ask someone who lived along the highway for a jug of water for his radiator. At this pace, he had to find about ten more kind strangers to give him enough water to keep his engine from seizing up.

When night fell and the winds were howling, they pulled off the highway at a community that must not have had more than a hundred people. Wade went into the only building with lights on—a washateria. He asked a lady who was drying her clothes where he could find a mechanic. (I guess she wanted clean clothes to wear after everything in her community was blown away!) She pointed down the road and told him, "If you go about half a mile, you'll find Elwin's. He's the only mechanic near here."

Wade and his friend drove slowly because the temperature gauge was in the red again. When they got to Elwin's, they realized it was long past normal working hours, but when they blew the horn, Elwin came out of the house next to his shop. Wade explained the situation, and pleaded, "I hope you can help me."

It soon became obvious that Elwin had been preparing for the hurricane by steeling himself with his favorite beverage—an ample amount of his favorite beverage. He looked a little unsteady, but he told Wade, "Yeah, okay. I'll see what I can do." When he opened the hood, a billow of steam rose into the night air. "I'll replace the thermostat, and we'll see if that does it."

When a customer complains, he is doing you a special favor; he is giving you another chance to serve him to his satisfaction. You will appreciate the importance of this opportunity when you consider that the customer's alternative option was to desert you for a competitor. —Seymour Fine

---

While Elwin was working on the car, Wade's friend motioned for him to walk a few steps away, and he whispered, "You know he's got you, don't you?"

Wade asked, "What do you mean?"

"He can charge you any price he chooses because you have nowhere else to go!"

"Oh, man, I hadn't thought of that."

A few minutes later, Elwin rose from the bowels of the engine, grabbed a watering can, and filled the radiator. He said, "Start it up, and let's see what happens."

Wade started the engine, and the temperature didn't rise above the normal range. When he turned the car off and got out, it was the moment of truth. He asked Elwin, "I really appreciate it. How much do I owe you?"

Elwin rubbed his face with his grimy hand and told him, "I ain't gonna take advantage of nobody. How about $50?"

The measure of our kindness isn't when people are nice to us, but when they're buttheads.

Wade was both relieved and grateful. Elwin could have taken advantage of Wade's predicament, but he treated him with a large measure of kindness. Wade told me, "I've never forgotten how Elwin treated me that night. His kindness and generosity meant more than just fixing the problem with the car—as important as that was. Now, that's great customer service!"

I have an employee I love to call "Mother Goose." Every time you're in our office, you feel like she wraps you up in a warm blanket right out of the dryer and gets you a hot cup of cocoa on a chilly day. She's that loving, and people love to be cared for by her. The best part is that she means it, and it shows. Can all of us move several notches closer to her example? Yes, but some of us will need to "fake it till we make it." Whether it comes naturally or not, it's important, so give it a try. You'll find out that genuinely caring for people brings great satisfaction—to them, certainly, but also to you.

When I fly (not skydiving but staying in the airplane!) the attendants always stand at the front door of the plane, smile, and say to almost every person, "Thank you for flying with us." They may be having their worst day in history, but their warm reception means something to me.

To be sure, some customers can be a pain in the butt, but if we treat them like adversaries, they become adversaries. As a business owner or manager, exemplary customer service is the main artery where the lifeblood of profits flows. The measure of our kindness isn't when people are nice to us, but when they're buttheads. If you can be gracious when they're frustrated with you, you'll build a great company.

IF YOU DON'T PUT THE CUSTOMER FIRST, CONGRATULATIONS—YOU'RE WELL ON YOUR WAY TO FAILURE.

At the end of each chapter, you'll find a few questions designed to stimulate deeper thinking and perhaps conversations with people on your team. Don't rush through these. You don't get extra points for speed!

THINK ABOUT IT

1) What are some memorable times when you were the recipient of outstanding customer service? How did the experience affect your view of the company?
2) When have you suffered from lousy customer service? Did you stay with the provider? Why or why not?
3) How would you describe the pressure to produce numbers in your company?
4) What are some ways you can redirect that pressure toward being an advocate instead of an adversary?

Don't they know? Don't they have a clue that we hired them to work like dogs so we don't have to? We don't need to give them directions, much less a vision, clear goals, and a job description. They just need to do what we tell them to do at that minute. They get paid, don't they? It's none of their business that we take two hours for lunch and leave early on Friday to play golf or go fishing. We don't pay them to take breaks and goof off. If we don't like their attitude, we'll show them the door! And bonuses at the end of the year? That's a laugh. We're the bosses, and we deserve it all.

CHAPTER 2
"MY EMPLOYEES STINK!"

Teamwork is so important that it is virtually impossible for you to reach the heights of your capabilities or make the money that you want without becoming very good at it.
—Brian Tracy

Bosses who are buttheads to customers are invariably buttheads to employees. It just works that way. As I've mentioned, employers, owners, and managers feel a lot of pressure to hit the numbers, and sometimes, they pile that pressure on the producers—the ones who connect with vendors and customers. What's behind this top-down pressure? Often, it's survival; the company's margins are so thin that if production doesn't rise, it's over. Or it may be comparison; bosses don't want to go to conferences or see buddies at the golf course and feel inferior. But it can also be raw, unalloyed greed; they're putting the squeeze on employees for their own gain. Now, I'm not saying it doesn't matter that the company is skating on thin ice, that we don't want to look successful when we talk to our friends, or that making money is evil. None of those things are absolutely true, but they can become the dominant motive in our relationships with those who report to us . . . and when that happens, we poison the well.

I'm afraid some of the managers who have been placed over me would say, "Tyler is the worst person at his job on the face of the earth!" To be honest, sometimes they would have been right. I'm not sure how it works in all industries, but I've noticed that some companies find "a company jumper" for new management positions, or maybe it's a struggling salesman looking to stabilize her income by getting out of commission-based sales and into a monthly salary with an exciting new management title to add to her resume. These people acquire the power to enforce company rules and regulations, along with personal agendas, and if they haven't been king of the world before, this is their chance to wear a crown and hold a golden scepter. Change can be really hard on a team; new management means new goals, new personalities, new mojo, new directions, and new visions. It's like starting over. This can happen in virtually all companies, including the one I'm truly grateful for and the people I proudly get to work with.

LEARNING THE HARD WAY

When I started my business, I had a lot to learn about hiring and managing employees. I hired my first staff member, who was twenty years old, at minimum wage for four hours a day. For the first couple of weeks, she was outstanding—prompt, attentive, excellent with customers, and great with follow through on assignments I gave her. She began coming in fifteen minutes late, then after a week or so, it was half an hour past the time she should have been in the office. Then, one morning at about 11 p.m., I got a text message from her: "Not coming in today." I thought, *Yeah, no kidding. You were supposed to be here two hours ago!* Even then, I gave her the benefit of the doubt—I assumed it was an emergency, a one-time thing. It wasn't. For the next four weeks, she came in when she wanted to, which was about half the time. I tried over and over to talk to her about how important it was to be reliable. Each time, she agreed and said it wouldn't happen again . . . until it did. Finally, I had to tell her it wasn't working out, and I had to let her go. She was furious. That was several years ago, and when our paths cross today, I can tell she's still upset with me.

Shortly after that dumpster fire, I hired another lady to work in my office. I let her start before the drug screening results came back because she assured me she was clean. She wasn't. Strike two. I thought, *Oh, geez, what am I doing?*

Years ago, a good friend gave me some really good advice: "Tyler, when you hire somebody, imagine how it's going to go when you have to fire them." He taught me to be much more selective and careful on the front end. If, for instance, I hire my wife's best friend and it doesn't work out, what happens to the relationship between the two couples? How do we respond when we see each other in the grocery store, at parties, or at church? What will it do to my wife's relationship with her? Will she be forced to choose between us? (In case you don't know, the correct answer is, "Yes!")

I've known business owners who treated their employees like pieces of equipment. If they produced and met expectations, these owners didn't say much, but if they fell behind or made a mistake, the message was clear: "Unless you change your act,

I'm gonna fire your sorry ass!" In many ways, I get it. I know the pressure of meeting quotas, so it's easy to see employees as productive machines instead of flesh and blood people. More times than I care to remember, I've heard owners boast, "Hire the masses and fire their asses." That's especially common in sales industries or departments.

> **Culture is about performance and making people feel good about how they contribute to the whole.—Tracy Streckenbach**

I had a conversation with a lady who has a staff of eight people. She wanted to talk to me about getting the most out of her employees, but I sensed we had very different agendas. I told her, "I want to hire people who become friends, so I can work with friends and encourage those friends. On our team, we support each other vocationally, emotionally, relationally, spiritually, and every other way."

She looked shocked. She shook her head and told me sternly, "My employees aren't my friends. I don't want them to be my friends, and I have no intention of being their friend." She paused for a second and then said, "Tyler, this is business. They have a job to do for me, and they'd better do it well, or I'll find someone else. When I walk into my office, I'm in charge. We're not a family. We're a business. When they come to work, they need to focus on their jobs and not worry about hurting anyone's feelings." This last part she said with a distinct note of contempt . . . mostly for me, but probably also for anyone on her team who tries to be a friend to another employee. (I imagined all her former employees with their heads on top of poles behind her office . . . or maybe just scalps.)

I knew there were people like her in the business world, but thankfully, there aren't that many who take it to such extremes. I decided to push back: "Do you not care about them as people? Are you interested only in their performance? How can your team serve customers with kindness and excellence when all you care about is meeting quotas? Is that really all that matters to you?"

I hoped she'd mellow, but instead, she dug in. "That's right. That should be all that matters to them because, at the end of the day, that's all that matters to me."

Yikes! I wanted to distance myself from this hot mess, and I felt truly sorry for anyone starting a career with her.

Do you think these employees sense the boss's perception of them? Of course, they do.

Now, when owners call me in to consult with them, one of my first questions is, "What's your average staff tenure?" This tells me all I need to know about how people feel working for this person. When people leave, demanding owners blame it on the employee. "She was never one of us," "He's been slacking since he got here," "I gave him a shot, but he didn't measure up."

TRUST IS THE GLUE

Relationships at work matter . . . they matter a lot. But we have to be intentional about creating and building trust, so people don't spend half their time looking over their shoulders to see if anyone is out to get them. Trust is the glue in every relationship, even in business. In a *Forbes* article, "The Essential Importance of Trust: How to Build It or Restore It," Dennis Jaffe comments:

> *Trust is often lost when we feel hurt by another's action and believe that this action (or inaction) was intentional. But by sharing our feelings with the person who hurt us, we might begin to see things differently and realize that their intention was not what we imagined. This may repair the breach quickly as misunderstandings are unraveled and communication deepens. It may be difficult to initiate such a conversation, however, given the tendency to withdraw when we feel hurt. Still, a person who is able to do this will find that they are less frequently hurt.*
>
> *In the same way, if we feel that we have done something to lose the trust of another, we can seek the other out and inquire about what has happened. True, this can feel awkward and risky—especially if one is a leader, parent, or person of authority—and this is not something that comes naturally. But this willingness to be vulnerable can ultimately lead to greater trust because the other person feels that their own vulnerability and needs are being respected. . . . What's helpful to remember is that trust is an ongoing exchange between people and is not static. Trust can be earned. It can be lost. And it can be regained.*[4]

Office culture can range from inspirational to sluggish to toxic. Leaders who create an inspiring environment cultivate trust based on understanding, collaboration, clear goals, and a compelling purpose. People are rewarded for courage and creativity, and failure is seen as a stepping stone on the path of growth. Those who aren't productive receive additional training and perhaps an assignment aligned more closely with their strengths. Employees love working there, and applications for open jobs come flooding in.

Leaders of sluggish cultures often have lost their sense of mission, so organizational energy ebbs or is diffused into projects that aren't essential. Sometimes, the vision is still crystal clear, but relationships are tense. People spend a lot of time jockeying for positions in every discussion instead of supporting one another and looking for creative solutions. Bosses and employees tolerate each other, but that's all. They complain . . . about everyone and everything, and they create secret alliances for support. (I believe most companies fall into this category.)

If sluggish cultures aren't corrected, they can become genuinely toxic. Every day at work is like multiple armies (the secret alliances) attacking one another. People feel used, creativity is condemned, and they live for Friday at 5:00. Bosses have very high expectations of employees, but they don't provide enough direction, resources, or encouragement. People seem chronically angry . . . or withdrawn in fear . . . or eager to suck up to get a word of approval. The employers can't keep their best people, and if they hire sharp people, they leave as soon as they figure things out.

Last year a good friend of mine exceeded every sales quota he was given, with the expectation of a promised bonus. His direct supervisor was happy with his numbers but let him know no bonuses were available this year. "Maybe next year." The supervisor told him that if he had made the effort to sell more and put in more hours, bonuses would have been offered. Clearly, his efforts weren't respected. My friend is currently looking for a new job.

In an inspiring culture, everyone looks forward to coming to work. They show up in a sluggish culture with at least some hope they can make a difference, but those who suffer in toxic environments dread walking through the door each day.

An MIT Sloan Management Review conducted a meta-analysis of many workplace studies and found that more than 90 percent of CEOs and CFOs believe improving their corporate culture would increase financial performance, and over 80 percent admitted their cultures aren't as positive as they wished they'd be. However, nearly all of those 80 percent said the leaders of their companies weren't investing resources to change the culture. "Lack of leadership investment was, by far, the most important obstacle to closing the gap between cultural aspirations and current reality." Toxic cultures create significant problems for employees, including an increased incidence of anxiety, depression, and burnout, as well as a 35 to 55 percent increase in serious diseases, costing the company healthcare benefits and lost productivity. About 10 percent of employees in the studies said their workplace is toxic. "Even companies with healthy cultures overall typically contain pockets of toxicity, due to abusive managers or dysfunctional social norms among certain teams."[5]

OXYGEN

If you're the leader of a sluggish or toxic culture, you're not alone. A lot of us realize we need to put ourselves and our teams on oxygen to revitalize our cultures, but many of us are still clueless. If you assume your culture is inspiring, you might need to think again. Bosses almost invariably overestimate their positive impact on their teams. (How's that for encouragement!) So put on your big-boss pants and have some frank conversations with people on your team, individually at first, and then together for you to share how you've failed (or at least, how you haven't succeeded as you thought). Then . . .

Model honesty.

Whether you like it or not, employees are looking to you as a role model. If you haven't been a good one, they've either followed your specific bad example, or they've found other ways to express their displeasure. You don't have to tell them everything, but you need to move the needle toward appropriate vulnerability. Not sure where the needle should be? Talk to leaders who have great cultures and find out.

Communicate appreciation.

Actress Celeste Holm remarked, "We live for encouragement and die without it—slowly, sadly, and angrily." Become your team's biggest cheerleader, but be sure it's genuine. (Nothing kills culture like phony praise!) Be specific, not general. Don't say, "You're great!" Instead, say, "Jennie, when you took care of that problem, I was amazed at how calm and thorough you were. That was a huge help to me and the team. Way to go!" How much appreciation do people need? There should be some form of it in every meeting.

Invest in development.

One way to say, "I value you," is to invest in someone's professional and personal development. Courses, books, conferences, continuing education, training for new technology, and all kinds of other information and skills can make your employees sharper, brighter, and more in tune with your big vision. (More on this in a later chapter.)

Keep the vision clear.

Speaking of the vision. We may have begun with a crisp, carefully constructed vision, but it can atrophy, eroding away day by day until all that's left is a list of tasks to accomplish. At least once a quarter, do a "vision checkup" to be sure yours is getting progressively clearer and more inspiring—for you and every person on your team.

In an article in *Entrepreneur*, Nav CEO Levi King uses the metaphor of a pail with a hole in it. Each employee is a pail. Leaders and managers (and parents) need to realize that early drips are often followed by an increasing pace of leakage. He insists that it's not enough for the leader to have a compelling vision or purpose:

You are responsible for keeping those vision pails full.

After all, you're the source of the vision, like a wellspring is the source of a stream, no matter how the stream twists and turns and takes on a life of its own. It's easy for you to refill your own vision pail. Your business is your baby; it's close to your heart all the time. If your pail keeps leaking regardless, think of how it must be for your employees. Our job as leaders is to always be looking for authentic moments in which to communicate our vision to our people.[6]

Align roles with strengths.

Don't simply hire people because they're available, and don't try to fit a square peg in a round hole. What do I mean? It's this: service people usually aren't great at sales, and salespeople often aren't talented in service. If you buck their innate talents, they'll be miserable, and so will you.

It's a pipedream to expect each person to have a perfect fit for their roles on the team. If they align at 80 percent, that's pretty fantastic! But people and organizations aren't static: the vision, products, and processes morph over time, and people may grow in skills or decline in capability. Stay focused and do a regular assessment. You might need to promote someone, move someone to another role, equip someone to do the role more effectively, or tell someone their time is up.

Keep your door open.

Cultures fester in the dark. When leaders don't listen well, suspicions multiply. You might need to invite some of the quieter people to share their perspectives with you, and you might need to limit the time you let gabby people talk. Listening is a key component of a healthy culture.

Multiply culture models.

It's absolutely necessary for you to be the prime mover in creating a dynamic, healthy culture, but as you do, you'll find others who follow your lead and become great models, too. Pour yourself into them, give them resources to help them grow, and then release them to lead wherever they fit best—inside or outside your company.

Simon Sinek remarked, "It's better to endure the discomfort of the truth now than to suffer the discomfort of the lie later."[7]

A LITTLE HUMILITY, PLEASE!

In his book, *Good to Great*, Jim Collins described the very best leaders functioning at "Level 5 leadership." He says that they:

> Display a powerful mixture of personal humility and indomitable will. They're incredibly ambitious, but their ambition is first and foremost for the cause, for the organization and its purpose, not themselves.... The good-to-great leaders never wanted to become larger-than-life heroes. They never aspired to be put on a pedestal or become unreachable icons. They were seemingly ordinary people quietly producing extraordinary results.[8]

This is the kind of person others want to follow. This is the kind of person they'll give their all for. This is the kind of person they want to become. In an article for *Forbes*, Merkle Global Chief Marketing and Communications Officer, Erin Hutchinson comments:

> Great mentors share their secrets to success. They are open not only about their wins but also about lessons they've had to learn the hard way. They're quick with a word of advice or encouragement. They help others steer clear of the obstacles along their path or at least give them a heads up about obstacles to come—even when they can't be avoided. And they model skills that often aren't taught in a classroom but are extremely valuable to your

career, such as accountability, teamwork and how to treat people with respect.[9]

And to drive the point home... in an article in the *Harvard Business Review*, the authors point out:

Humility and gratitude are cornerstones of selflessness. Make a habit of taking a moment at the end of each day to reflect on all the people that were part of making you successful on that day. This helps you develop a natural sense of humility, by seeing how you are not the only cause of your success. And end the reflection by actively sending a message of gratitude to those people.

The inflated ego that comes with success—the bigger salary, the nicer office, the easy laughs—often makes us feel as if we've found the eternal answer to being a leader. But the reality is, we haven't. Leadership is about people, and people change every day. If we believe we've found the universal key to leading people, we've just lost it. If we let our ego determine what we see, what we hear, and what we believe, we've let our past success damage our future success.[10]

This is a warning each of us needs to hear.

REDNECK IQ TEST FOR BOSSES

Those are plenty of quotes and insights from respected leaders. Now it's time for me to tell you something I learned from being a crappy boss. I'll frame it in the form of an IQ test for redneck bosses:

Wherever you are right now—at home in your favorite chair, at work killing time, or sitting with a fishing rod in your hands—stand up and examine your hands to be sure they're in good working order. All good? Good. Now, make a concentrated effort to find your butt. Some of you may need to use both hands. If you've found it, you've passed. I've seen many employees, managers, people in sales, and owners who couldn't find their butt with both hands. Don't tell anyone, but sometimes I have trouble in that department myself! You can sit down now.

You may find this to be an obnoxious and silly exercise but let me apply it this way: No matter what your role in the company today, there's another rung up the ladder. Whether you're the president, CEO, or royal potentate, you've got your eye on a bigger company or a more wealthy country. But many of you are so dense that you couldn't find your butt if you used both hands! You're consumed with the wrong metrics, ruining your culture, and driving off your best people.

Don't you dare assume you're "self-made."

I couldn't be more grateful for some bosses who saw that I was drowning while being circled by sharks and jumped in to save me... or I would have been a gourmet lunch for several maneaters!

Some of those perceived maneaters are clients or lack thereof, company policy, competition, management, colleagues, and lack of product knowledge.

These people helped me succeed, but first, they had to rescue my faltering career.

If you're successful, you didn't get there on your own. Particular people believed in you when others didn't; they opened doors that seemed impenetrable, and they spoke faith and hope to your soul when you thought of giving up. Don't you dare assume you're "self-made." None of us is. Every day, take time to be thankful. Your gratitude list may be the same day after day, but that's fine. Repetition reminds you where you came from and who carried you along, and you need all the reminders you can get! I've known people whose success went to their heads (and hearts). They acted like their crap didn't stink. Don't be one of those people. Another part of the daily analysis is the recognition that you're still an idiot in more ways than you want to admit. Your friends think your jokes are dumb, people on your team have strengths you don't possess, and news flash: you're often not the smartest person in the room. You may be the face of the business, but the real work is done by those behind the scenes. Honor them.

Depending on the type of business you're in, you may have management and regulators looking over your shoulder every day. Are they advocates or adversaries? It's often hard to tell. More times than I can count, those in the corporate office have dropped the hammer on me for what looked like no good reason at all. I have to remember that I don't have all the facts and details. I'm the soldier in the trenches, not the one who's back at headquarters receiving intel from all over the battlefield. There are accounts of American GIs who fought in Belgium in December of 1944 and saw tanks roll by and planes fly overhead. For days, they sat in the freezing cold, hearing the sounds of war in the distance. It was only later they learned they'd been part of one of the great battles of the war: the Battle of the Bulge. Sometimes, I feel like those wet, cold, confused soldiers. I'd like to say that I've learned my lesson, but you'd draw a different conclusion if you saw my reaction to the latest "industry directive from on high."

Our team members are carefully watching our attitude. Do we complain at the drop of a hat? Do we blame others for every problem? Do we make excuses like, "It's a tough market right now," "The interest rates are too high," "Our vendor is a fool," "Our products can't compete in the market," or, here's the kicker, "I don't know why our culture isn't inspiring everybody! What's wrong with these people?" The more you focus on the negatives, the more toxic your culture will become. Count on it.

I'm a first-class blamer. My instant reaction to any problem is pointing my finger, especially if it's a sticking point with the corporate office, but I'm an equal opportunity grouch. Here's the deal: my success isn't dependent on other people, products, or programs. I have to take responsibility for every situation, the boom times and the lean years. I have to watch my assumptions. When I hear about someone more successful than me, I look for "reverse excuses," advantages they had that I didn't: their daddy's money gave them a head start, they live in a rich community, they took over a thriving business, or some other reason they're doing better than me. But hey, I'm not a victim of their success. I'm only a victim if I see myself as one and practice mental gymnastics to drag them through the mud.

For a long time, I failed the redneck IQ test, but eventually, I found my butt. It's right here.

What's my greatest asset as a business owner? My team. My job is to put them in the best position to excel, and then celebrate every win like we're Little League champs. And I have to tell you, I work with the best people ever. I don't just work with them and they with me. We care for each other's success in every way. Most of them didn't come to me looking for a job. I already knew them, I knew their character, and I had a hole I knew they had the skills to fill. But it was character first, skills later. I tell people regularly that I'm just the pretty face of the business, but they are the muscle! Truthfully, they're both.

For a long time, I failed the redneck IQ test, but eventually, I found my butt. It's right here.

WHAT IF THEY ACTUALLY STINK?

I'm all for self-expression, but only up to a point. I'm not sure if it's Gen Z or more widespread in our culture, but I've walked into offices where I felt like my presence was an inconvenience to the people hired to serve me. We need to look at every person on our teams through the eyes of our customers.

One of my neighbors retired recently. He made an appointment with an investment firm to roll over a sizable 401k. When he opened the door, he was greeted by the receptionist. She smiled and welcomed him, but he couldn't get over her nose ring, left arm sleeve of tattoos, a streak of red in her hair, and clothes that were more appropriate for . . . he couldn't think of anywhere they'd be appropriate. As he waited to be walked into the office of the financial planner, he kept thinking, *Am I going to put my entire career earnings in the hands of someone whose first-line employee is Goth?* He listened politely to the ideas of the executive, but he had already made up his mind: he wasn't going to put his money there. He found another investment firm.

I'm not saying that people shouldn't be creative and authentic. Those are very good traits, but business owners need to be aware of how customers and clients feel when they interact with people on their team. I'm looking in the mirror here because I guarantee you that I've lost some clients because I often dress in nice jeans and high-end cowboy boots, but they were looking for a suit. When they saw me, they made an instant decision to take their business somewhere else.

So, you may be asking, "Hey, Tyler, are you dumb? If you're losing customers by the way you dress, why don't you wear slacks, a tie, and shoes normal people wear?"

I'd reply, "This is what normal people wear in the ranchlands of Utah. The folks who are looking for a suit aren't from around here." Is that just an excuse for not wanting to change? Maybe.

Appearance matters, and it matters to your bottom line as well as your reputation. Think about it: if you forked over a considerable amount of money to attend a wealth-building seminar, and the guy who walks on stage is wearing cutoffs, a ragged shirt, and flip flops, with a week-old beard and bed head, would you be excited about listening to him, or would you listen for the sound of your $500 being flushed down the toilet?

A hallmark of a healthy creative culture is that its people feel free to share ideas, opinions, and criticisms. Lack of candor, if unchecked, ultimately leads to dysfunctional environments. **—Ed Catmull**

Mormon founder Brigham Young famously said, "He who takes offense when no offense is intended is a fool, and he who takes offense when offense is intended is a greater fool." In other words, I'm not trying to offend anyone. Don't judge me. I'm just inviting you to take a hard look at yourself and those you lead to see what you're communicating to people who meet you for the first time. Are you so caught up in "being your authentic self" that you're losing clients? I'm afraid that's true of me, at least to some extent. What's more important: insisting on your unique expression or appealing to your customers? I've gotten a lot of traction in the right circles because I don't try to fool anybody about who I am, but when I look back at my career, I quickly realize my greatest nemesis, the one who has torpedoed me more times than I can count, is the guy looking at me in the mirror. But my image is consistent with the vast majority of people who live in my area. They're looking for a guy who understands farming and ranching, along with estate planning, and helps with investments and financial goals that run deep in middle America, as well as the needs of small businesses, but my style and manner don't appeal to everybody.

Our clients' perception is their reality, and their reality determines their purchasing choices.

IF YOU DON'T HONOR YOUR EMPLOYEES, CONGRATULATIONS—YOU'RE WELL ON YOUR WAY TO BUSINESS FAILURE.

THINK ABOUT IT

1) Think about the span of your career. Were any of the organizational cultures inspirational? Were any sluggish? Were any toxic?
2) What lessons did you learn from each experience?
3) What are some ways trust is built in your present work environment? How is it eroded? What part do you play in the health of your team culture?
4) What difference would it make for you to do a better job of:

    Investing in development?

    Keeping the vision clear?

    Aligning roles with strengths?

    Keeping your door open?

    Multiplying culture models?
5) What does the appearance of people on your team say to customers?

You've trusted people in the past, and it was a disaster. The only smart thing now is to trust only yourself. You know better than anyone else anyway. Don't give them any room to make their own decisions—they'll only screw it up! Tell them exactly what to do, how to do it, and when to do it. Don't leave anything out. And remember, every employee is high risk, so hire the very minimum of staff members. They're expensive, and they make far too many mistakes. Before long, you'll have to fire them anyway, and that's always so awkward. It's better to just do everything yourself.

CHAPTER 3
"IF I WANT IT DONE RIGHT..."

If your business depends on you, you don't own a business—you have a job. And it's the worst job in the world because you're working for a lunatic!
—Michael Gerber

My business has two sides: property-casualty insurance for home and auto and life insurance and investments. My income is based on a complex algorithm, based on new business I bring in and keeping the clients I have. The company has a built-in incentive for me to write new business. If I bring in more clients and write bigger policies, the algorithm rewards me, but if I'm happy coasting at current levels, I get knocked down. Our customers don't realize that if ten different agents wrote their policies, each of the ten would receive a different compensation based on the agency's algorithm.

Why am I getting into the weeds about the intricacies of my compensation? To give you a window on two people: me and another agent, whom I'll call Myron. The growth in my business is the product of outstanding team members serving people with excellence and kindness day after day. My name is on the sign, but they are the real stars of the show. Myron has a different management philosophy: he insists on doing virtually everything himself, and as I'll explain, it has cost him a bundle of money.

Myron answers every phone call, even when he's out meeting with someone, and he handles every piece of paper that his work generates. He doesn't want his employees to have any responsibility because he's sure they won't do as good a job as he would, so he doesn't train them, he doesn't respect them, and he certainly doesn't encourage them. He's afraid that if he lets someone else interact with a client, something bad will happen, and he'll lose the business.

Either he doesn't realize it or he doesn't care that no one wants to work for him. People in the community have concluded he's odd because he's such a perfectionist, his business hasn't grown as much as it could have, and he's leaving an enormous amount of money on the table.

I've tried to enter his life to point out his counterproductive beliefs and behavior, but each time, he has insisted he has to be the contact person for every client—no exceptions. I've tried reasoning with him, explaining how our office functions, and helping him see the pros of change and the cons of remaining immovable. He has blown me off every time.

His algorithm is probably around half of what it could be. I've done a quick calculation that over the last twenty years, Myron's intransigent perfectionism has cost him about $4 million in gross agency income. If anything, I think that number is low. If he had hired eager, competent people, would it have cost him money? Yes, for salaries, training, and office equipment. But each one would have brought in many times what they cost. Entrepreneurs know there are two kinds of employees: cost centers and profit centers. Hire profit centers, train cost centers to become profit centers, and if they can't make the change, you'll need to swallow hard and make a bigger change for them.

Self-reliance becomes a hindrance when it becomes the only way we function.

Why would someone make such expensive choices? They may articulate their resistance in different ways, but at the heart of it all is fear—the fear of losing complete control, failure, overextension, or trusting others with your reputation and finances.

Certainly, there are times, like the first months of a startup, when business owners have to do a lot of work themselves to get the venture off the ground. I get that. I experienced that. However, self-reliance becomes a hindrance when it becomes the only way we function.

After the startup phase, some business leaders can't make the shift to hiring, training, and delegating to competent people for the team. They insist on having every decision go through them. They micromanage their people. The effects are similar to radical self-reliance because the cause is the same: the fear of letting go, the fear of trusting people and having them fail us.

A *Forbes* article about this problem states that micromanaging is often a form of bullying, making "employees feel disenfranchised, humiliated, belittled, and their mental health deteriorates." The article quotes Nora Robinson, PR rep for Refresh Remodeling, who said that "micromanagers often resort to bullying tactics with the belief that it makes workers more productive, but it's because they don't know how to manage their team effectively. Oftentimes, these bosses view burnout as the price for productivity."

How widespread is the destructive impact?

- 79% of employees said they'd been the targets of bosses who micromanaged them.
- 71% said it interfered with their performance at work.
- 85% said their enthusiasm for the job was affected.
- And 69% considered changing jobs.[11]

Don't tell people how to do things. Tell them what to do and let them surprise you with their results.—General George Patton

---

The disease spreads like this: micromanagers invariably focus on mistakes instead of achievements and weaknesses instead of strengths. It doesn't take a psychologist to understand the impact on team members—they *feel* belittled because they *are* belittled, they lose confidence in themselves because the boss has communicated that he doesn't have confidence in them, and their performance suffers under the barrage of messages that shout, "You're not good enough!" "I can't trust you!" and "I wish I'd never hired you!" In this environment, creativity is crushed under the hammer blows of criticism. Are you a micromanager? Let's see . . .

- Do you dictate how people spend their time getting the job done?
- Do you reject input from people on the team and insist you know more than them?
- Do you delegate and then oversee even minute details?
- Do you require virtually all approvals to go through you?
- Do you believe having compliant team members is more desirable than creative ones?
- Do you feel uncomfortable with these questions?

ACCOUNTABILITY . . . FOR WHAT?

Leaders who micromanage trust only themselves—and maybe not even themselves! They're afraid their people will fail too often, too badly, or too publicly. Yes, we need to hold people on our teams accountable, but as much for innovative thinking as for checked boxes on a to-do list. When our people feel we believe in them, they do better work.

In a *Forbes* article about the importance of accountability, John Hall cites an alarming study by author and leadership expert Anne Loehr:

> *Ninety-three percent of employees don't even understand what their organization is trying to accomplish so they can align themselves with that goal. Additionally, 85 percent of leaders aren't defining what their employees should be working on. And 84 percent describe themselves as "trying but failing" or "avoiding" accountability, even when employees know what to fix.*

The lack of accountability creates increasingly bigger problems, but creating a culture of trust, truth, and integrity encourages people to own their mistakes without fear, so they can learn from them (which, in case you haven't noticed, is what this book is about!). This positive culture, Hall asserts, improves employees' performance by encouraging ownership of the process and the product, and ultimately, it has an impact on the bottom line. He cites another study:

> Gallup found that highly engaged workforces outperform competitors *and result in 21 percent greater profitability. As business coach Jason Blumer* puts it, *bringing in a healthy level of accountability can keep "the ideas flowing and the execution happening"* From my experience, that's the simplest and most effective way to grow your company.[12]

SEA CHANGE

Some business leaders read a chapter like this or listen to a podcast and are instantly motivated to make changes, but most of us need more prodding and tools to help us change. Let me offer some advice:

1) Remember, it starts with you.

Nothing changes unless you change. Your team is already following your lead and responding (or reacting) to your style of leadership. Don't shift the burden of change onto them. It's on you. It's all on you. The first step is to be brutally honest with yourself.

2) Find a professional coach, mentor, or honest friend.

The next step is finding someone who will coach you through the process of reclaiming your role as a great leader. You'll need someone who is willing to tell you things you don't want to hear but who is solidly on your side as a cheerleader. Most of us are simply following the example of a flawed person who was our boss. To change, we need to hang out with a gifted, wise person who is a far better role model.

In an article for *Forbes*, Merkle Global Chief Marketing and Communications Officer, Erin Hutchinson comments:

> Great mentors share their secrets to success. They are open not only about their wins but also about lessons they've had to learn the hard way. They're quick with a word of advice or encouragement. They help others steer clear of the obstacles along their path or at least give them a heads up about obstacles to come—even when they can't be avoided. And they model skills that often aren't taught in a classroom but are extremely valuable to your career, such as accountability, teamwork and how to treat people with respect.[13]

3) Have a "come to Jesus" meeting with your team.

When you're ready, call your team together and share what you've discovered about yourself. Give pertinent examples, and don't defend yourself. Vulnerability takes a lot of courage, so muster as much as you need, borrow courage from your coach, and wade in.

4) Apologize.

When we take responsibility for our flaws and mistakes, two things happen: people are amazed and a barrier to trust begins to crack. Be honest and direct: "When I do this, it's wrong. I'm so sorry. Please forgive me." No excuses, no blame-shifting, no rationalizing.

> *Wouldn't it be a refreshing experience for your staff to hear you say, "That's on me. I own that mistake. I'll do better"?*

I'm not sure of the psychology of upper management, but I've noticed that very few top leaders are willing to apologize for mistakes. It's almost taboo. It's as rare as hens' teeth. Wouldn't it be a refreshing experience for your staff to hear you say, "That's on me. I own that mistake. I'll do better"? Fear stops most leaders from showing any chinks in their armor. They don't want to show weakness in any capacity. When someone has the audacity to challenge a decision or even ask a simple question, they go into full-on defensive blitz! Guns blazing! What kind of leadership is that? Not the good kind.

5) Explain that things are going to be different.

An apology is essential, but it's not enough to build (or rebuild) trust. Words don't mean much; people need to see, smell, taste, and feel that your management style is changing. Commit to listening more, value creativity, and focus on strengths. Explain that you're still asking for excellence, but you're learning to trust them to have the same goal. George Patton was the Commanding General of the US Third Army during World War II. He was known for his no-nonsense approach to leading his men, pushing them to accomplish what others thought was impossible. But he wasn't a micromanager. He said, "Never tell people how to do things. Tell them what to do, and they will surprise you with their ingenuity."[14]

Talk to each person on the team about the best way to delegate responsibility and authority, clarify roles, and show your support. If someone needs to be placed in a different role, explain the reason clearly. When you hire people, don't settle for a warm body to fill a slot on the organizational chart. If your office culture is inspirational, competent people will beat your door down to join the team. I've heard that in college basketball, good teams recruit, but the elite teams select the best from all those who want to be there. Be the leader of an elite team.

6) Create a feedback loop.

In the early stages of this transition, it's especially important to give people the opportunity—regularly and often—to give you feedback on how you're coming across. You'll probably find that some people trust you fairly quickly, but others are slow to buy the new product (the new, improved you) you're selling. A feedback loop lets people know you're still on the learning curve, which helps to build trust.

7) Look for progress.

Not perfection. For each of us, our leadership style, including our values, beliefs, and behavior, has been shaped over many years, even if we're young. Real change takes concerted effort, tenacity, and time. Don't be surprised when you find yourself falling back into old, toxic, self-reliant, and micromanagement patterns. It's going to happen. Just stop, reassess, and choose to be a leader others want to follow.

> **No person will make a great business who wants to do it all himself or get all the credit. —Andrew Carnegie**

One of the most powerful things we can do as bosses is offer to help those who report to us. We should position ourselves as coaches who are dedicated to the employee's success. We don't hover over people to notice any weak point so we can pounce to fix their problem. Instead, we wait until they ask for our assistance (which only happens if they trust us to help and not hurt them in the interaction), or if we see someone is struggling, we step in with an offer to help, but first listen ... and listen even more ... to the person's diagnosis of the problem and the intended solution. Even with the best of intentions, things can go sideways. In the *Harvard Business Review* article "How to Help (Without Micromanaging)," the authors warn:

> *Even if the timing is right, intervening can go wrong when it isn't clear why you are getting involved. Managers play a lot of different roles, and their responsibilities include evaluating employees and doling out rewards and punishments. This power dynamic can get in the way of effective help. When bosses step in, their involvement can imply that people are messing up in a big way. That's why employees often hide or downplay issues and fail to solicit guidance. They can become unreceptive to the assistance, defensive, or demoralized, which hinders creativity and performance. Therefore, as a leader at GlowDesign told us, managers must be careful "not to go in there and create*

> so much anxiety that you're in a worse spot.... It can be like 'Here's the boss, and gosh, he's really unhappy with what we're doing.'"
>
> Because seeking and receiving help can make people feel so vulnerable, managers need to clarify their roles when intervening in employees' work. They should explain that they are there to help, not to judge or take over. They need to foster what Amy Edmondson, a professor at Harvard Business School, calls *psychological safety*—an environment in which interpersonal risks are encouraged.[15]

We are relational creatures, and we function best in connections built on trust and respect. Every relationship has its messy moments, but the best ones find ways for people to understand and appreciate each other. That's my job as a boss... and it's yours too.

I don't know anyone who doesn't struggle with the tension between self-reliance and trust in others. As business leaders (or those who aspire to be), we can't dodge our problems. We have to look them square in the eye and find ways to overcome them. In *The Obstacle Is the Way*, Ryan Holiday is brutally honest about our default responses to problems, but he offers hope that the problem itself shows the way forward:

> This thing is in front of you. This issue. This obstacle— this frustrating, unfortunate, problematic, unexpected problem preventing you from doing what you want to do. That thing you dread or secretly hope will never happen. What if it wasn't so bad?

What if embedded inside it or inherently in it were certain benefits—benefits only for you? What would you do? What do you think most people would do?

Probably what they've always done, and what you are doing right now: nothing.

Let's be honest: Most of us are paralyzed. Whatever our individual goals, most of us sit frozen before the many obstacles that lie ahead of us.

Holiday reaches back to the emperor-philosopher, Marcus Aurelius, who wrote a journal entry never intended to be read by anyone else, but full of wisdom that applies to all of us:

Our actions may be impeded . . . but there can be no impeding our intentions or dispositions. Because we can accommodate and adapt. The mind adapts and converts to its own purposes the obstacle to our acting.

The impediment to action advances action.

What stands in the way becomes the way.[16]

IF YOU INSIST ON DOING IT ALL YOURSELF, CONGRATULATIONS—YOU'RE ON THE ROAD TO BURNOUT AND BUSINESS FAILURE.

THINK ABOUT IT

1) What are the benefits and liabilities of toxic self-reliance?
2) Do you know anyone who fits this description? What's that person like? What impact does he or she have on others?
3) Do you agree or disagree that fear is at the root of toxic self-reliance and micromanaging? Verbalize your answer.
4) Look again at the elements of a "sea change." What would happen if you followed this advice in leading your team?
5) What's the obstacle to your leadership?

Professional development is a waste of time. All that time invested, and for what? Very few clients ask about your credentials anyway. And the "training" . . . such a colossal bore! Lectures aren't interesting and group meetings are only interesting to see what asshole tries to impress everybody. Only marginally entertaining. No thanks! I don't even like those people. They just want to hear themselves yak endlessly to a captive audience. I've never been to a conference that didn't require some serious nap time . . . and neither has my buddy Chad. (Yes, Chad, I still have those pictures in case I need to blackmail you.)

CHAPTER 4
"CONTINUING ED. IS FOR SUCKERS."

There's no shortage of remarkable ideas, what's missing is the will to execute them.
—Seth Godin

The world is divided into two distinct groups of people: learners and laggards. Learners soak up every ounce of information, skills training, and the wisdom of experts. They read books and articles, find the best podcasts, take notes, talk to peers to clarify what they're learning, and then take steps to apply the principles. These are the people who provide outstanding service to customers and clients, impress their bosses, and leave the laggards in the dust. I don't really need to describe *them*. They exhibit the opposite of the traits and commitments I described in the lives of learners.

Training and experience are the two wheels of the success bicycle. If either one is missing or flat . . . you get the idea. Learners have identified the X factor and put it into practice. At conferences or on

Zoom calls, many employees down an energy drink, so they can stay focused. They take notes and gladhand (or glad-verbally-greet) their peers and bosses, but when they get back to work, the insights and directives escape their brains like water through a sieve. (If you're a city person and you don't know what a sieve is, look it up.) Every industry invests heavily in advanced training for their staff, hoping they'll apply just a fraction of what they hear, so they'll be more productive and the company will be profitable, keeping the doors open at least a little longer.

> **Yesterday's home runs don't win today's games.** —Babe Ruth

You've probably attended your share of regional or national conventions. You check in at the hotel and sit through several days of high-energy motivational speakers and grass-roots, detailed training. You reconnect with old friends and meet new ones, so you can have pleasant mealtimes. In the meetings, sitting around hundreds or maybe thousands of peers, you laugh at the jokes and clap when speakers are finished . . . while you text buddies about the utter boredom of it all. In the middle of the forty-seventh talk (at least it seems like that many), your mind drifts to think about the family vacation you're planning, the fishing trip you're going to take, the plumbing repair that's going to cost a fortune, the new golf clubs you want to order, the latest row with your spouse and kids, the conversation with the waitress at last night's dinner when you asked and she told her story of being a broke single mom, and anything else that promises to keep you awake until the break when you can have another cup of coffee and another high-calorie snack. Another talk or two, and then . . . the dreaded "assigned lunch groups." You greet everyone with a smile, hoping you can either say something really witty or fade into the wallpaper. Your secret hope is that you can pull off the charade and say, "Hey, sorry, but I have to take this call." That's after you texted your admin back home and told her to call you right away.

Long afternoon sessions, then a high-profile speaker that evening. In every meeting, you notice people writing in notebooks, Googling books recommended by speakers, ordering marketing materials, subscribing to a podcast, and downloading a video that promises so many new clients that you'll double your income in six months!

Day 2 isn't as exciting as day 1. You didn't sleep well last night and combined with the travel and downing more food than the 1,000-pound sister, you sleep through the late morning and afternoon sessions. Oh, you're in your seat with a pen in your hand, but you're gone . . . just gone. In those intervals when you're aroused by laughter or clapping, you take some time to check social media and your favorite website. You catch a few sentences from the speaker. It sounds interesting but not *that* interesting. You drift off again. At the end of each talk when people are clapping, you join in with all the zeal of a puppy.

Day 3 is spent planning to leave early enough to get the rental car back before the onslaught of others who are thinking the same thing. You're thinking, *I hope my flight has movies—really good movies. Why* doesn't every airline provide earbuds? I hope whoever sits next to me isn't like the last guy. He smelled like over-ripe goat cheese!*

You get home utterly exhausted. Your spouse asked, "How was the convention?" And you say, "Great. Lots of terrific speakers. Met a lot of people. Great. Just great."

The next day at the office, you unload the stack of papers from the event. You tell yourself, *I'll sort all this out later when I revise my business plan, but right now, I've got a lot of fires to put out.* But later never shows up. You certainly can't work on it now because three days of calls, texts, and emails are straining the capacity of your technology. You quickly triage all of them to handle the urgent ones first. After a few long, packed days, you're finally caught up. Now you're thinking about next week, next month, and all the reports and appointments you already have on your schedule. The content of the conference becomes a distant memory. Day after day, those pesky conference notes sitting in the corner of your desk remind you every day that you didn't follow through on your commitments. After they begin to grow mold, you slip the notes into the round file next to your desk.

But hold on a minute. Let's go back to the event for a minute. What did the company shell out to host it—speakers, facilities, food, and all the rest? Many companies have a division dedicated just to pull off events like this. That's corporate money, but what about *your* money? How many Benjamins did you add to your credit card bill? How many hours were you away, not making new contacts and not massaging connections with existing clients? In other words, what were the opportunity costs? How did your staff team function while you were away? How much did you drink while you were gone? How much are you keeping secret from your spouse?

Something had to change, and that something was me.

So... what's the point of it all? How many learners were there who were lapping up every idea and encouragement? And how many laggards were there wasting time and money because they didn't apply much of anything when they came home? Was it worth it? Really? Did you need another gift bag of key chains and knickknacks, and maybe an ugly T-shirt? Before you completely misunderstand me, let me explain: Many of the people who attend these events—and pay attention during them—are high producers or are committed to becoming high producers. They've either been learners for years or are starting their careers as learners. The event is primarily for them, and it's very successful. Oh, there are plenty of laggards who show up (and if I offended you by using "you" in my description of how laggards experience corporate conferences, I'm only sorry if you're not one of those). But other laggards don't see any benefit in attending. They make all kinds of excuses: "It costs too much," "I'll be away from my family too long," "I don't get anything out of those events," and on and on. For them, there's always an excuse... for avoiding training, wasting time, not following up with clients, not investing in staff, and failing to take advantage of every opportunity the company offers.

If you assume I'm coming down hard on laggards because I consider myself to be superior, let me disabuse you of that idea. I know a lot about laggards because I was one of them—a card-carrying, blue-chip version. In the early years of my career, I believed the company name, our great products, and my good looks would attract masses of people to my doors. (Well, maybe not my good looks.) Our office drifted along. We got some new clients, but we lost others. I was making a living, but certainly not knocking it out of the park. Then, one day I got sick and tired of being mediocre. I began to notice the excuses that dominated my thinking, and they made me want to puke. Zig Ziglar called this "stinkin' thinkin'." I was mired in "good enough." Mediocrity was entirely normal. I had small dreams and no fire. Something had to change, and that something was me.

I had suffered a financial rock bottom a few years earlier and climbed out of the hole, but this was just as (and maybe more) serious—it was a career rock bottom. They say alcoholics and addicts don't change until they hit that point. Before then, there's always another excuse; it's always someone else's fault. But no more excuses, no more blaming others. I had created this muck of a career, and I had to find a way to climb out.

That's why this book is about failure. I'm an expert—experienced and tested. But I finally realized my assumptions had made me think and act like a victim. No one is sure who first said it, but it's true: "Insanity is doing the same thing over and over again and expecting different results."

By that definition, I had been insane. No, people in white coats didn't show up to put me in a straitjacket and cart me away to an asylum, but it was insanity nonetheless. I had created a world of low energy, low expectations, and low income, but it was also a world of resentment toward those I perceived were getting in my way and jealousy toward those more successful than me (which was a long list of people).

Now, when I reflect on "my insane years," I see a lot of people in business with the same disorder. They want to succeed—and they expect to succeed—but they aren't willing to put the work in to be better at what they do. Will the curve be steep? Probably. Will they fail along the way? Certainly. The path to success has many stepping stones to failure. Will it be worth it? Absolutely!

In my younger days, I lived for adventure. I worked on a 7,000 cow-calf operation as a working cowboy—it was awesome! We were always on horseback and riding hard. We had to trade horses daily to keep fresh mounts under us. One day, after a long day punchin' cattle, I was riding a young colt, teaching it the finer points of ranching. I mentioned to an older and wiser cowboy riding next to me, "This horse is 10 percent better than he was this morning!"

Aim for incremental success. Each step, no matter how small, is actually a huge step in the right direction.

He smiled and asked, "Really? Does that mean in ten more rides just like today, he'll be perfect?"

That really stuck. Even if that colt got 1 percent better every day, he wouldn't be perfect in one hundred days. The same is true for you. Don't shoot for perfection. It'll drive you (and everyone around you) crazy. Aim for incremental success. Each step, no matter how small, is actually a huge step in the right direction.

One of the most important resources for gaining sanity and success is finding the right coach or mentor. Don't look for "the golden boy" or "girl" for whom success seemed to come effortlessly; instead, look for someone who learned the hard way, wading through the swamp of trial and error with their boots on. You'll learn more from people like this than those who claim to have had all the answers from the time they were born. (In fact, be very suspicious of anyone who makes fantastic claims and offers easy paths to success. That's a load of crap . . . and you can quote me.) But don't misunderstand. I'm not suggesting that you hitch your horse to someone who has struggled their whole career. I'm recommending that you find a partner who is a learner, whose mistakes and failures have resulted in greater wisdom and success. Some coaches excel in relationships—others in systems and efficiency. Figure out what you need and who can help you, and do whatever it takes to learn from that person.

This advice is for a much wider audience than business owners. No matter where you are in your career and whatever line of work, call high-producing experts and invite them to lunch. Sure, they make a lot more money than you, but the cost of lunch can produce priceless results. I've taken many successful restaurant owners to lunch in their own restaurants. Even when I was starving and they were essentially retired, I recognized the value of their wisdom. Successful people keep growing because they never stop learning. Be a sponge. Arrive with specific questions, and say the smartest thing anyone will ever say: "Tell me more about that." There's always more to learn because even in the same industry, demographics, economic factors, and culture affect how we do business, so drill down past the concepts to practical applications. And for Pete's sake, do what they recommend you do. If you can't bring yourself to take this step, stop reading, throw this book in the trash, and get a job commensurate with your bottom-feeding expectations, hopes, and dreams.

ROADBLOCKS: REAL AND IMAGINED

I'm not saying there aren't real challenges when we want to pursue professional development. There are several, but in the vast majority of cases, the benefits far outweigh the risks or costs. Some common roadblocks include:

1) The cost

A study called "Upskilling at Scale" found that 40 percent of those surveyed said the biggest barrier to professional development is the cost.[17] If companies pay all the expenses, this problem is solved, but if they pay only part, the barrier may still be there, just not quite as tall.

2) The fit

Some employees are unsure where they're going in their company or their career, so they're hesitant to take courses that sharpen their skills in a particular function. Sometimes, it's not the employee who's unsure; it's the boss who isn't clear about the employee's role.

3) The time

Most of us have a hard time squeezing everything into our schedules now, especially if we have children who, as they grow up, have different but equally consuming calls on our time. If we're moving up the ladder in our companies, the bosses often expect us to put in more time at work. How can we add something else? More than a third of employees reported they "don't take professional development courses because they feel like they're too busy at home or at work."[18]

4) The future

Some employees don't feel their jobs are secure, so asking for time and money to develop their skills seems like a big risk. If they take this step, their supervisor may assume they're actually looking for a job somewhere else, and they're using the company's time and money as a springboard to something better.

If you're a boss or manager, pay attention to this: if you don't provide opportunities for professional development, you're going to lose some of your best people. A study of 1,200 office workers found:

> *Nearly 6 in 10 (58%) respondents say they are likely to leave their company without professional development or continuing education and career training to develop new skills and drive career advancement. . . . When asked how likely they are to leave their employer if they don't receive*

development opportunities, women, people of color and Millennials reported being more likely to leave. According to the findings, 61% of women and 55% of men would leave. In addition, 68% of black, 70% of Hispanic and 80% of Asian respondents indicated they would leave, compared with 53% of white respondents. By generation, 66% of Millennials and 63% of Gen X indicated they would leave, while 47% of Baby Boomers would.[19]

WHY NOT?

I could list a dozen reasons personal development benefits you and the company but let me focus on just a few. First, for you. Professional development...

1) Revs your engine.

You may have been bored out of your mind in some classes in high school and college, but when you picked your electives, you were far more motivated. Professional development targets specific knowledge and skills to open doors of opportunity, which fills our tanks with high-octane gas!

2) Enlarges your vision.

When you learn from the best in your field, you're exposed to high-level thinking, so your imagination can soar. You begin to see yourself succeeding in ways you hadn't envisioned before.

3) Sharpens your thinking.

These courses aren't designed as "an easy A." They challenge you to think more clearly, ask better questions, and search for the best solutions.

4) Makes you indispensable.

You were valuable to the company before, but now you're much more valuable. You're becoming an asset management relies on.

5) Impresses the boss.

Your enthusiasm, insights, and skills gleaned from the coursework aren't hidden underground. People notice, especially those who are looking for people to promote.

6) Builds confidence.

Does professional development make people into arrogant snobs who believe they're better than anyone else? It can, but it shouldn't. As you gain understanding and get a better grip on successful practices, you'll definitely improve your performance, but you'll also realize how many people contributed to that success. You'll be both confident and grateful . . . a beautiful combination.

And for the company, investing in professional development of the staff . . .

1) Shows your commitment.

When you invest time and money in the development of people, you're making a bold statement about yourself, the company, and the team members.

2) Raises expectations.

It's natural: everyone expects progress from those who have taken advantage of the company's investment.

3) Adds a spark.

Those who have taken courses and/or been coached inevitably have fresh ideas, more optimism, and a higher level of energy.

4) Improves productivity.

The bottom line is that the price companies pay for professional development is worth it. Employees will be more effective in their existing roles or equipped for a bigger role.

5) Facilitates team building.

In most courses, interaction with other students is an integral part of the training. Participants learn to collaborate, resolve conflicts, and encourage each other. Back with their teams, they bring these new skills to every interaction.

6) Deepens the pool.

Good executives are always looking for more people who show leadership potential. One of the best ways to test someone's interest and capacity is to send them to a development course and see what comes from it.

Even if you are on the right track, you'll get run over if you just sit there.—Will Rodgers

---

Professional courses in personal development have a far greater impact than merely reading an article or sitting in a meeting for an hour or so because concentration over time does something really remarkable: it changes our brains. People a lot smarter than me call it neuroplasticity. New thoughts and actions, and especially focused and repetitive ones, cause the brain to reorganize by forming new neural pathways. Psychologist Ilene S. Cohen explains:

> *Brain plasticity means that our habits, behaviors, and thought patterns can change over time, reinforcing the idea*

> *that personal development is an ongoing process. With consistent effort, we can reshape our brains to develop new skills, adopt healthier habits, and overcome limiting beliefs. . . . Personal development is not a destination but a continuous path through self-awareness of what needs to change. It requires commitment, effort, and patience, along with a willingness to see what we are up against in our most profound relationships.*[20]

Those of you who know me well are now thinking, *Where did Tyler find this? Does he even have a brain?* Yes, I've even been known to use it from time to time, and the amazing news is that it's changing and growing! Gradually, very gradually, new ways of thinking and acting become second nature. It's like learning to play the violin or learning a new language. At first, there's a steep learning curve—everything feels awkward and, well, wrong! But you become a little more comfortable with the bow and the strings, or you remember a phrase or two. Then you make a little more progress, and a little more. If you stop working at it, you go back to square one, but if you keep it up, sooner or later you'll play well enough to impress your family (who are very supportive), or you can at least find the bathroom in a foreign country and order at a restaurant. That's progress!

Your brain's ability to adapt is a superpower! Every step forward changes a few pathways deep inside your cranium. As you begin to pursue professional development, fight through the urge to give up. Stick with it, and it'll come more naturally.

CORRELATION

For employers, it's important to correlate professional development for employees with the values of the company. When these align, employees quickly understand how to apply new principles to the existing culture. When they don't align, employees' confidence in the company deteriorates. In an article for the *Harvard Business Review,* Patrick Lencioni observes that too often, companies publicly state their values only because they believe they need to, not because they mean anything to the executives or employees. He explains:

> *The debasement of values is a shame, not only because the resulting cynicism poisons the cultural well but also because it wastes a great opportunity. Values can set a company apart from the competition by clarifying its identity and serving as a rallying point for employees. But coming up with strong values—and sticking to them—requires real guts. Indeed, an organization considering a values initiative must first come to terms with the fact that, when properly practiced, values inflict pain. They make some employees feel like outcasts. They limit an organization's strategic and operational freedom and constrain the behavior of its people. They leave executives open to heavy criticism for even minor violations. And they demand constant vigilance.*
>
> *If you're not willing to accept the pain real values incur, don't bother going to the trouble of formulating a values statement. You'll be better off without one. But if you*

> have the fortitude to see the effort through, you can learn some important lessons from the few companies that have adopted meaningful corporate values. Whether their values stemmed directly from the vision and character of their founders or were developed later through formal programs, these companies all followed four basic imperatives in creating and implementing their values.

Lencioni warns that unless you're willing to follow this advice, it's better not to have stated values at all because "poorly implemented values can poison a company's culture."[21] Think about this before, as, and after you send people to courses for professional development.

ONE MORE PLUG

This topic has been tremendously important in my life and my career. I wish I could say I was a learner in high school and college, but I wasn't. In fact, I felt repulsed by some of my college profs in business school. They were telling me how to run a business and how to become wealthy using principles of economics and the finer points of accounting, but they were getting by on a teacher's salary. Again and again, I thought of the saying, "Those who can, do, and those who can't, teach." My lofty educational goals were to make Cs and take Fridays off. I didn't care what I learned; I just wanted to get my sheepskin at graduation. (I'm more than a little embarrassed to admit this, but I told you I'd be honest with you.)

When I began my career, I suddenly became an avid learner. I wanted to understand the inner dynamics of the world of business, so I read everything I could get my hands on. (If my profs had seen me, they'd have fainted.) One day, I came across a single sentence that changed the trajectory of my life: "The knowledge and wisdom you gain by increasing your intelligence shouldn't be used primarily to traffic in money but to improve people's lives." Wait a minute! Is that true? Haven't people always wanted more money to fund their comfort and pleasure? Gordon Gekko was a despicable character, but aren't we all just like him? Maybe . . . maybe not. "The better angels of our nature" (to borrow from Abraham Lincoln) change our motives from self-serving greed to care for others. Is that even possible in the world of business today? Yes, it is. Did you know that Elon Musk, one of the richest people in the world, open-sourced his Tesla patents, so others could use his technology and build on his knowledge base? Musk is on one end of the spectrum. On the other are countless men and women who use their platform in business to serve customers, clients, and team members. They are, to borrow a term, "shepherd leaders" who have found a way to blend creating a great business with creating a great life.

I have a prime example of this blend living under my roof. My wife, Tiffany, became a nurse practitioner and received a doctorate in the field. What was her motive to earn a doctorate? There was no extra money involved. The pay scale was the same without the doctorate, but she wasn't driven by money. She simply wants to serve people with as much expertise and care as she possibly can. When I drift away from this blend, talking with her—and even thinking about her—brings me back.

Do you have someone like that in your life?

Are you that someone in others' lives?

IF YOU AREN'T ATTENDING COMPANY MEETINGS, SHOWING UP AT CONFERENCES, STUDYING INDUSTRY NEWS AND EVENTS, AND GETTING INVOLVED IN STUDY GROUPS, THEN CONGRATULATIONS—YOU'RE ON THE ROAD TO MEDIOCRITY AND FAILURE.

THINK ABOUT IT

1) Review the roadblocks to professional development. Which of these, if any, is a real problem for you? How can you overcome it?
2) Why do you think so many people leave companies where they don't find opportunities to develop their skills and broaden their knowledge?
3) Which of the benefits for individuals is most motivating to you? Explain your answer.
4) Which of the benefits for companies seems most attractive? Explain your answer.
5) Whom do you know who lives with a blend of genuine care for others and professional skills? What about that person is attractive to you?
6) What's your next step in pursuing professional development?

Here's the deal: we live in a dog-eat-dog world. There are just so many customers to go around, and I intend to have my fair share . . . actually, I intend to have more than that. To reach my goals, I need to look good by making the competition look like losers. I want their market share, and I'll do anything to beat them. Hey, it's not just me. Everybody is cutthroat. You either kill or be killed. It's my job to make sure people understand my competitors lie, cheat, and steal, and their products are garbage. But it's not just "those guys" at the other company. I'm also competing against people in my company, so they're fair game too. They're idiots. They don't know the business like I do. And besides, they're trying to steal my customers. I need to grind them in the dirt before they do that to me.

CHAPTER 5
"HE'S MINE!"

The twin killers of success are impatience and greed.
—Jim Rohn

A friend of mine runs a regional sales office for a national investment firm. He told me about an explosion that blew things apart where he works—no, not an IED planted in the parking lot. This was a relational bomb that shattered the working relationships. One day, a client called a sales rep at the investment firm he had been using and asked to speak to his advisor (I'll call him Will) to invest a large sum of money. Four years earlier, Will had set him up with automatic withdrawals from his checking account, and the money was invested in a mutual fund. Now, he was retiring early, and he had been given a generous retirement package. When the investor called, Will was out, so the call was routed to Molly, who was relatively new at the firm. Molly was eager to make things happen for this man . . . and especially for her career . . . so she didn't bother to check to see who had been his wealth manager. She explained how his $2 million could be invested in relatively safe stocks and bonds to provide for him and his wife throughout their retirement. Her suggestions were just what he was looking for, and he signed all the forms before he left the office.

The next day, Will got a notice that the order had been placed, and he saw Molly's name on it. He could have calmly walked into her office and said, "Molly, I think there's been a mistake. Today's sales report says that an investment was placed by you, but you know that I'm the rep for that client. Please fix that for me." But instead, he walked down the hall to rip her head off! He yelled at the top of his lungs, "Molly, what were you thinking? You stole my client!" When he turned the corner and stormed into her office, he didn't miss a beat: "You'd better make this right! Right now!"

Successful people are always looking for opportunities to help others. Unsuccessful people are always asking, What's in it for me?—Brian Tracy

---

Molly growled, "If you'd been here, you could have served the client, but you took a long lunch break. It's your fault you weren't here. He appreciated how I served him! Now shut up, and get out of my office!" She had been under the gun to get her numbers up because she was never going to qualify for the company-sponsored vacation if she didn't get credit for this sale.

Will wasn't finished. He had more bombs hidden away. He stomped out of Molly's office and into the sales manager's office (I'll call him Lee). He was on a call, but Will interrupted and began demanding that Lee at least reprimand Molly (or even better, fire her) and give him the credit and commission for the sale: "You've got to fix this!"

Lee spoke to the person on the phone, "I'll get back to you in a few minutes," hung up the call, and turned to Will. His issue, Lee instantly realized, was DEFCON 3 and could easily escalate to DEFCON 1! "What's up?" he asked.

Will explained the situation, the order Molly took, his request for her to make it right, and her reaction, and he repeated, "You've got to fix this!"

"I'll take care of it," Lee assured him. "I'm sure it's just a misunderstanding."

Will barked, "It's NOT just a misunderstanding!"

"Wait here," Lee said as he waved his hands in a way meant to reassure him. "I'll talk to Molly and get this worked out."

Will sat fuming in Lee's office. His delay coming back wasn't a good sign. When he finally walked back in, Molly was with him. Lee may have been thinking of Rodney King's famous plea when he was being beaten by police: "Can't we all get along?"

It was obvious neither of them wanted to follow his advice. Will snapped, "Yeah, we can get along—as soon as Molly admits she stole my customer!"

Will repeated his gripe about Molly. He looked hard at her and then at Lee, and then he reminded Lee and Molly that the client had asked for him by name.

While Will had been waiting, he mentally surveyed his list of all the ways he could get Molly fired, but the meeting with Lee left him more than dissatisfied. He decided to call the client and make sure he knew that Molly was not his representative, and in the future, he should speak to him and him only when making a transaction. But Will wasn't finished. He then requested that the client call Lee to confirm that he was his rep, not Molly. Will then made it a point to let the client know that Molly wasn't that good at her job and probably wasn't going to be with the company very long anyway.

The whole thing blew up because the client was so freaked out by the experience that he found another firm and transferred his account.

Greed is poison. Don't drink it.

Lee was horrified, but he hoped the problem would blow over. It didn't. The relationship between Molly and Will was chippy when it wasn't frigid. For months, they plotted each other's professional death. Finally, Molly found a role at another company.

Competition over sales isn't inherently a bad thing as long as the competitors have goodwill toward one another. But far too often, the desire for abundance combined with the fear of scarcity drives people to unethical means of driving up their numbers. Bottom line: don't treat others in your company like garbage, and don't treat customers like stepping stones. Greed is poison. Don't drink it. I'm saddened by people who check reports to make sure they are "winning" before they do anything else when they get to the office. When stealing clients is part of the game plan, you've lost sight of what's important. When winning contests under any circumstance feeds your ego, you have become a monster.

Do you think people notice greed in themselves? I've talked to people who admitted character flaws of all kinds: lust, adultery, gluttony, lying, bullying, cheating, and many others, but I've never heard anyone say, "You know, Tyler, my problem is greed." Greedy people don't realize they have become greedy. I usually see a great salesman who gets carried away by the thrill of the kill. They think they are just fantastic at their job, but unfortunately, people get in their way, and then heads roll. They can't wait for the recognition they deserve and believe they are entitled to be seen as industry royalty. I would venture to guess that right about now, you're thinking of one of your colleagues, aren't you? Go ahead and admit it. How many of your colleagues are thinking this of you?

Do you think other people notice greed in us? Not always, but when they do, their respect for us goes in the toilet. They may not identify it as greed, but they can smell it on us. They detect that we talk too much about money, possessions, pleasure, comfort, power, and getting what we want at others' expense. These messages may be subtle, or they may be as plain as day. Greedy people . . .

1) Are self-absorbed.

Who do they love to talk about? Themselves. What do they talk about? Their power over others, their achievements, and their valuable possessions. When are they bored out of their minds? When the subject isn't on them.

2) View others as competitors or pawns.

Greedy people have an internal and vivid pecking order. Every person in their lives either is a competitor who knocks them down a notch or is surpassed in triumph... or one of "the little people" who are used (and abused) to help them move up.

3) Show little empathy.

Greedy people are so self-possessed that they don't care about the hurts and needs of others, even if they cause them. When others are steamrolled by their demands and abuse, they shrug it off as just part of the game. But actually, they may fake empathy if it impresses others.

4) See every encounter as win or lose.

Every deal and every conversation is a test of strength, and they hate to lose! They have to be seen as the smartest, richest, most competent, wittiest, and best-looking person in the room. (That, as you may recall, was the way the Enron execs were described!)

5) Believe they deserve success.

Greedy people have the attitude of the title of this chapter—they believe every customer should be thrilled to do business with them, every banker should fall at their feet and give them all the capital they want, and the community should put them on a pedestal (and maybe hold a parade for them every year).

6) Are never satisfied.

Over a century ago, John D. Rockefeller turned a fledgling oil business into Standard Oil, the largest and most powerful company in the world, becoming the richest man on earth. In an interview, he was asked, "Mr. Rockefeller, what will it take for you to be satisfied?" He responded, "Just a little bit more."[22] He was known as a religious man and a philanthropist, but behind the scenes, he was a cutthroat businessman who drove countless others out of business. Have you ever seen someone fire a family member over a lost sale of a gross amount of six bucks? I have. It's insane. How in the world did that business owner get to that point?

IF IT'S YOU

Does the description of some or all of the six traits feel like you're looking in a mirror? If you suffer from the disease of greed, the first step is to be ruthlessly honest. Great businesses are built by great people, those who put others first, including employees. Great people, in my experience, are those who are grateful for every person who helped them and every break they got along the way. Let me give another warning: I've known some business owners who went hunting for rabbits when an elephant walked by! They became far more successful than they'd dreamed . . . and far more than they deserved. Instead of being humbled and grateful, they acted like it was all due to their brilliance. There's nothing in the world wrong with internal satisfaction in a job well done (which is the right kind of pride), but there's something very wrong with arrogance and greed. I've seen some of these people become sloppy, cutting corners, and crossing all kinds of ethical boundaries. They assumed they were "above it." They weren't. The truth came crashing down like a sledgehammer, and everything they worked for was smashed to bits. It didn't have to be that way.

I don't think you can be any more of a butthead than me, and if I can change, so can you.

Am I tempted to fudge sometimes? Do I think all the ethical requirements in our industry are a pain in the butt? Yes and yes, but I keep some people in mind, men and women who crossed the lines and paid a huge price. A friend of mine says we gain wisdom in three different ways: Some of us learn from classroom lectures or reading a book. Some of us learn by looking at the consequences of the mistakes of others. And, some of us don't learn anything until we suffer the consequences of our own mistakes. Very few of us are in the first category, more in the second, but I'm afraid most of us are in the third. I'd say this: at all costs, avoid the fourth category—failing to learn at all!

Each of us has the God-given capacity to learn, grow, and change. I don't think you can be any more of a butthead than me, and if I can change, so can you. But good intentions aren't enough. Do the hard work of self-analysis to uncover greed and arrogance, feed your soul with wisdom and gratitude, and find someone to walk with you on this journey of being a glad servant instead of an insecure tyrant. Small and simple steps eventually produce terrific results.

We might wonder what's underneath greed and arrogance. Well, it depends. Some people feel terribly insecure and compensate by being tough, crushing those who get in their way, and rewarding those who are blindly loyal. For these people to change, they need to be honest about their insecurity and do the hard work to uncover the cause. When they resolve the hurt, fear, anger, and shame that produced their defiance, they'll still be strong leaders, but with added dimensions of wisdom, gratitude, and compassion. But others are somewhere on the spectrum of personality disorders. They're wired to dominate, intimidate, and manipulate, and they genuinely don't give a damn who gets hurt in the process. The first kind of person may well read a book like this. If they do, they'll be defensive when they read this chapter, but at least some of them will see the benefits of healing what has caused them to act out their insecurity by being a butthead. The second kind of person doesn't read a book like this. My emphasis on learning from failure and flaws seems totally ridiculous to them.

Three great forces rule the world: stupidity, fear, and greed.—Albert Einstein

---

Riches and power are addictive. Like any other addictive substance or behavior, we start by experimenting, and then we get hooked. As the addiction progresses, we experience "the tolerance effect"—it requires more and bigger wins, more and bigger possessions, more and bigger accolades to give us the same rush. (I was going to say more and bigger spouses, but that hits too close to home for some people!) Before long, our lives are totally consumed with more and bigger. The consequences are similar to an addict's:

our selfishness, lies, and foolish decisions ruin the culture of our teams, harm our relationships with those we love, and, when things finally collapse under the weight of our foolishness, our reputation is shattered. No, it may not happen soon, but it'll happen. As the saying goes, "Pride comes before a fall." It's inevitable, even if it's delayed. The news is littered with stories of men and women whose greed distorted common sense and led to colossal falls. For a while, they looked like superheroes... until it was discovered they were chumps.

Don't add your name to the list.

THE RIGHT "MORE AND BIGGER"

For me and everyone I've ever met, real fulfillment comes from having a purpose far bigger than ourselves, something that takes us out of our little world of selfishness and propels us to live for a greater cause. It can be almost anything: serving at a nonprofit, starting a nonprofit, mentoring at work, coaching kids, volunteering at your place of worship, caring for an elderly person, or participating in anything else that gets you out of yourself. It's not rocket science. In fact, you probably already know what floats your boat. Here are some questions to consider:

- What have you done in the past that gave you a strong sense of purpose?
- What knowledge, skills, and strengths can you invest in others' lives?
- What makes you angry?
- What touches your heart and makes you sad?
- What are several opportunities open to you right now?

- If you dreamed about making an impact, what would it look like?
- Who is doing that, or something like it? How can that person help you take steps forward?
- What's stopping you?
- What's the first (or next) step?

Are you surprised that I asked about anger and sadness as a window to your purpose in life? Our emotions tell us a lot about what matters to us. If our perspective on injustice, broken lives, unmet needs, and missed opportunities doesn't do something to our hearts, there's something wrong. We *should* get emotional! We *should* take action! I got this insight from a philosopher of the last century—Popeye the Sailor Man. When he got so frustrated he couldn't take it anymore, he burst out: "That's all I can stands. I can't stands it no more!"

What can you not stands no more?

IF IT'S SOMEONE YOU CARE ABOUT

So what do you do if a family member, friend, or person who reports to you seems to be infected with the disease of greed? Since it's very easy to excuse the problem because the lure of more is all around us, most people are instantly reactive and insist, "What are you talking about? That's not me!" So, should you wade in with guns blazing or hide behind your desk? Neither one. Consider one or more of these approaches:

1) Be honest about your temptations.

At the right time and in the right way, talk about your own struggle with wanting more, the temptations for a nicer car or bigger house, a more expensive vacation or a new set of golf clubs, or whatever entices you. Describe times you've failed and how you suffered the consequences, such as debt, loss of respect, worry about money, etc. The person may or may not grasp why you're sharing your story, and in fact, he may remark that it's too bad you have a problem with greed . . . because he sure doesn't! But you're planting the seed.

2) Hold up a mirror.

If you care enough to take a risk in the relationship, again, find the right time and communicate in the right way by holding up a mirror and saying, "Here's what I see in your life." Be specific, but don't raise your voice. Expect initial resistance, and perhaps continued hostility. Communicate that you're speaking up because you don't want to see her suffer the painful consequences you've seen in the lives of others.

3) Be realistic about the struggle.

If you get this far, you've made real progress with the person! People who see themselves as exceptionally powerful and competent usually don't have much patience for prolonged and uneven progress. If success can't be instantaneous, it's not worth the trouble! Explain that you want to talk about this a dozen times over the course of months (if the person is willing to stay engaged). The effort will be worth it, and change will have huge benefits in leadership, family relationships, a sense of calm and peace, and physical health.

4) Be there when the crash happens.

If none of your efforts are successful, be there for the person when their world collapses in a heap. Foolish, selfish decisions inevitably come back to bite people. For some, it takes years; for others, it's very soon. Broken relationships, divorce, a mountain of debt, bankruptcy, burnout, major depression, and other major calamities are loud wakeup calls, and the person will need support during the time of deep reflection on what really matters, how the path went in the wrong direction, and how to climb out of the hole.

Purpose, meaning, and love . . . those are the real riches.

German philosopher Arthur Schopenhauer observed, "Wealth is like seawater: the more we drink, the thirstier we become."[23] But it doesn't have to be that way. If we live to make a positive impact on people, we'll love them, serve them, and want the best for them, no matter how much money we have. And if, through skill or luck or a combination of things, we make more money than we need, we can pour more of our money—in addition to our hearts—into the lives of others.

Purpose, meaning, and love . . . those are the real riches.

I hate to say it this way, but if you're filled with lustful greed, this may be the only way to get through your thick skull:

IF YOU'RE A GREEDY BASTARD, THEN CONGRATULATIONS—YOU'RE ON THE ROAD TO PERSONAL, SOCIAL, AND PROFESSIONAL FAILURE.

THINK ABOUT IT

1) What are some ways greed shows up in business owners? What can be some of the consequences?
2) How does it show up in employees? And the consequences?
3) Look again at the six traits of greedy people. Do any of them ring true in your life? Explain your answer.
4) What are some ways greed is like an addictive substance or behavior?
5) If you were warning someone about the dangers of greed, what would you say?

I don't want to start my day that way, so I'll do something else. I don't even want to look at my to-do list. It's oppressive. Nobody cares that I take a little extra time for myself. I need to look at videos of those shoes to be sure I spend my money wisely. I know I told my client I'd call him back today, but I'm sure tomorrow is fine. I hate reports. I'd rather have a root canal than try to figure all this out on my own. Let's grab some coffee. We'll get back to work later. Hey, did you see the game on Saturday? The ending was amazing. Let me tell you about it.

CHAPTER 6
"THAT CAN WAIT 'TIL TOMORROW."

What you have to do and the way you have to do it is incredibly simple. Whether you are willing to do it is another matter.
—Peter Drucker

When people spend time with me, they can't imagine that I ever waste time. I'm a high-energy, can-do guy who's always on the go. At least, that's what I want people to think, but I can get distracted like anyone else. No, I don't play video games, but I love the rodeo, fishing, and hunting. I could sit for hours watching YouTube clips of ranch broncs, square body truck restoration, catching big smallmouth bass, and seeing a guy in camouflage take down a deer that qualifies for Boone and Crockett. But I'm too embarrassed to tell you more than that, so let me tell you about a man I hired for our insurance business. I'll call him Dick.

Dick looked the part. He was tall, young, and handsome with a winning smile. Everyone knew him. He had been a star basketball player in high school, married a beautiful girl, came from a prominent family, and was very well-connected in the community. He had worked for a competitor, so he already had his license. Getting him up to speed in our system would take very little time or effort. When he asked for an interview, I thought I'd won the lottery. I hired him on the spot.

I'm not the kind of person who micromanages. Nobody will accuse me of being a "helicopter boss." Dick had been officing out of his father's business, and he asked if he could continue that practice. I said, "Sure!" I wanted to give him some time to drive up the onramp of our business, so I was patient as he grew into the job. A couple of weeks went by, then a month. Each day, I called: "Hey, Dick. I hope you're having a great day! What's going on today? Give me a rundown of who's on your schedule."

And each time, I heard some version of this mantra: "Tyler, it's going to be a really good day. I've got a lot of leads and a lot of people on my call list. I'll be hammering on this in the afternoon, but I have to run home this morning for a little while. My wife needs me." He pauses to let that sink in and see how I respond, but before I can say anything, he changes the subject to something he knows will pique my interest: "Hey, did you see that monster buck that was shot last weekend? Man, it's a beauty!"

I'm slow, but I eventually catch on. For weeks, I assumed Dick was making up any time he spent at home (which I thought would be short so he could get back to work) by working longer hours. Wrong. The numbers didn't lie. He was only writing a few new policies, and the "lots of people on the call list" either were people he'd called before or didn't exist. When I finally asked, "What the hell is going on? I was counting on you!" he admitted he spent a lot of time surfing the internet, found any excuse to go home to see his wife, and went back to his office long past when he knew he could get something done.

Kicking the can down the road doesn't make the pain go away; it only reschedules it.

His pipeline of contacts and sales had closed tight, and his wallet was empty. As I mentioned in an earlier chapter, poor business habits create a lack of income, which results in dumb, self-destructive decisions. I had such high hopes for him, but he left my business and the insurance business entirely.

I understand the tug to take breaks . . . long breaks. I can burn an hour with the best of them, but I have enough discipline to know when I need to stop being distracted and get down to business. Don't judge me as a terrible boss. I made a solid, good-faith effort to help Dick succeed, but he couldn't commit to the necessary work. The moral of the story? Don't be a Dick! Kicking the can down the road doesn't make the pain go away; it only reschedules it. And like an untreated infection, it can get much worse.

A good work ethic is the best thing my parents poured into me. I want to work hard—and love my work. When work really sucks, I dig in harder. The pieces don't magically fall together for people who are lazy and undisciplined, even if you were a stud or a beauty in high school or college and have the right family name and status in the community. Dick had all that, and look where he ended up. Neither employers nor consumers care about how awesome you think you were in high school or college. They care about commitment. Do your job. Earn a good reputation. It will open amazing doors of opportunity.

According to one study, almost 35% of employees admit they go online to play games or shop during office hours, and 43% admit they spend too much time talking to others at the office when they should be working.[24] Other research shows that the average office worker experiences fifty-six interruptions a day, and 64 percent use social media and waste more than two hours a day on activities not related to work.[25]

> *Whatever you can do or dream, you can begin it. Boldness has genius, power, and magic in it.—Goethe*

Of course, it's unreasonable (and, in fact, impossible) for employees to be completely focused on their jobs from the moment they walk in until the moment they walk out each day. They need breaks to go to the restroom, grab some coffee, and get lunch. They may also have to travel for their jobs, so time in the car or subway (We don't have those where I live.) can be a time to relax from the pressure of work. And those who stare at screens all day need to give their eyes a break from time to time. All of these are normal and necessary breaks in the workday... but I'm not talking about those. I'm talking about not working when we should be. Let me list just a few intentional distractions:

1) Personal calls

"It'll only take a minute." That's what we tell ourselves and anyone else who's nearby. We forgot something at home, we want to connect with a friend, we're scheduling a dinner out, we're setting up an appointment with the doctor, or a thousand other things. I'm not saying these calls don't need to be made, but they can happen during downtimes like lunch or breaks.

2) Chatting with people at the office

Mindee wants to tell us all about her daughter's dance recital, and she includes every detail. Larry wants to talk about the fight he had with his wife this morning before leaving for work. Conversations are important, but again, we need to respect our company and our boss and have them at the right time and the right place.

3) Social media

"Just look at this!" To be honest, I've never understood the lure of cat videos, but I realize I'm in the minority. It's really easy to look at one image or post—personal, political, or whatever—and then scroll to the next one, and the next, and the next. Pretty soon, our minds are captured by the algorithms tailored to our browsing history, and we have difficulty refocusing on the job.

4) Games

Sometimes, these are just mind-numbing distractions, but they can also be fierce competition. Solitaire is quick and easy. Fortnite, Minecraft, Counter-Strike, and a host of others offer challenges that can occupy a lot of our time at work and at home.

5) Shopping or planning a trip

Online shopping has taken over the world of commerce, and the options are endless. We can view a hundred (or a thousand) different options for any product, each with particular specifications and price. It's tempting to upscale just a little, trying to rationalize why we need to spend just a little more for the next step up. We were sure it would only take a minute to pick what we wanted and make the order, but there were so many choices! And if we're thinking about taking a trip, oh, man, so many places to stay, so many perks at each place, so much to do and so many things to see. And then we have to communicate with everyone who's going.

6) Procrastination

"No hurry. I'll handle that tomorrow." Some people are habitual procrastinators. They regularly put off decisions and effort, hoping they'll feel more motivated later. For others, the problem is fear—they're afraid to fail and look foolish, so they find excuses to avoid any risk. Whatever the cause, procrastination lowers job satisfaction and raises the stress level for the employee and everyone else involved.

Sometimes, though, our environment works against efficiency. Factors in the office can distract us from productive activity. For instance:

7) Confusion about the task at hand

If the job description isn't clear, we can drift as we try to figure out what we're supposed to be doing. If we aren't sure who reports to whom, we can be preoccupied with worries about saying too much or too little to the people up and down the org chart. If the chain of command isn't clear, we may not feel like we can say "no" to others' requests for our time.

8) Meetings that are tooooo loooong

I can tell when a meeting I'm leading has gone too long when I see people fidget or their eyes roll back in their heads. As a leader, I need to make sure I'm prepared, the agenda is reasonable for the time allotted, I engage people in the discussions, and I keep things moving.

9) Meetings that are unnecessary

A friend told me he talked to a guy who works at a government agency, and the employee told him, "This week, I had more meetings scheduled than time in each day. They were overlapping, so I couldn't even go to all of them. The only thing I did all week was attend meetings. All my work was put on hold." My friend asked how often this happens, and he replied, "I probably spend half my time in meetings. About a tenth of them are important. The rest are a waste of time."

10) Burnout

It may seem like a paradox, but employees who are working too hard and under too much stress often feel overwhelmed and look for distractions.

11) Boredom

Maybe you hired someone who isn't intrinsically motivated, or maybe the company's vision and mission aren't compelling enough to keep the employee engaged. Whatever the cause, people who are bored at work find it easy to excuse their distractions because they're convinced their work doesn't really matter anyway. (And I hope that's not you!)

12) Too many emails and texts

We want to be informed, but really? I could spend half my day reading and responding to every message that comes to my phone. I have to do triage: answering some with careful reflection, answering others in a flash, delegating many to my team, and ignoring those that don't rise to the level of any response. But being this ruthless and disciplined is difficult and for many people, seemingly impossible.

13) Trying to fix something beyond your capability

I've seen people take days to work on a faulty printer or computer program when they could have called an expert and had it fixed in an hour. I appreciate ingenuity and diligence, but when you exhaust your expertise, call a professional, and invest your time in work you can actually do well.

14) The boss takes up too much time

Sometimes, the problem is at the top. I've talked to employees who are frustrated because their boss consumes too much of their day with small talk. Maybe the boss is lonely and needs some human connection, or maybe the boss has lost the vision and passion for the work. Maybe the boss's organizational skills may not be sharp, so he gives mixed signals when he delegates and fails to stay on top of progress, but he wants to talk endlessly about how things are going.

Instead of wondering when your next vacation is, you ought to set up a life you don't need to escape from.—Seth Godin

---

When Brett was in college, he applied for a job with the Corps of Engineers to look for encroachments across boundary lines at a large reservoir near his town. (This is me, too.) The job paid more than twice as much as any other work he could get for the summer, so he was thrilled when he received a job offer. He soon realized he'd stepped into a culture that was totally foreign to him. Brett had always been a diligent student and a dedicated worker in his summer jobs, but this was different . . . very different. He told me that it was frustrating (and confusing) because it was supposed to be an 8:00 to 5:00 job with an hour for lunch, but on the first day when he arrived a little before 8:00, no one was there. In fact, they didn't show up until 8:30. Very quickly, he realized the daily schedule was "flexible." People came in at 8:30 or later, went for coffee at a nearby restaurant at 9:30, walked back to the office by 10:30, and worked until noon. The lunch break actually wasn't an hour. It was at least an hour and a half. They worked from 2:00 to 4:00 and then went home.

After about six weeks of wasting so much time, Brett decided to take some initiative. He asked the supervisor if he could look at a section of the lake boundary by himself that day. When he came back the next morning, he listed fifteen encroachments. The entire crew didn't address that many in an average week, so when the district manager found out about Brett's proficiency, he had a very frank conversation with Brett's boss. Brett realized his initiative had been out of step with the culture of the office, and he promised he wouldn't be so bold again. For the rest of the summer, he was a good soldier and followed the lead of his boss. It was a lesson Brett would never forget.

A TEST

Take some time to answer these questions for yourself, and then ask people on your team to answer them privately. After that, have a good, honest conversation about being focused at work.

1) What are my most common distractions?
2) How easily am I distracted?

3) When and how do my priorities at work get cloudy?
4) What are our goals? How clear are they?
5) How productive are our meetings?
6) What can make them more productive?
7) Is there technology or a process that would make me more productive?
8) Do we schedule adequate breaks for personal issues and relaxing?

Bad habits—either yours or those who work with you—don't have to ruin careers. Habits can be changed, but only with a clear plan, tenacity, persistence, and accountability. Look beneath the surface to determine the real problem. Sometimes, it's a deep-seated fear that drives our behavior, but maybe the problem is that no one ever communicated clear expectations. Whatever the cause, wasting time is costly . . . to everybody.

THE OLD ADAGE SAYS, "THE ROAD TO HELL IS PAVED WITH GOOD INTENTIONS." IF YOU HAVE GOOD INTENTIONS BUT NO FOLLOW-THROUGH, THEN CONGRATULATIONS— YOU'RE ON THE ROAD TO FAILURE.

THINK ABOUT IT

1) Would you say that wasting time is a huge problem, a moderate issue, or no big deal for you? Explain your answer.
2) How about the people who work with you?
3) Which of the intentional distractions is most problematic? How does it affect you and/or the people on your team?
4) How about the problems created by your organization's culture?
5) Take the test. After you're finished, write down two or three things you learned about yourself and your team.

Oh, come on. Everyone lies a little . . . in business, with family, and with friends. It's just the way things are. If consumers knew everything about our products, they wouldn't buy them. They don't need to know every detail. And besides, I'm under pressure to meet my quota by the end of the month, so I may have to cut a few corners to get my numbers up. Shortcuts are fine if they work. No one will find out, and if they do, they'll just blow it off. And if I exaggerate a bit to impress people, that's entirely good, right, and normal. Get over it!

CHAPTER 7
"IT WAS JUST A LITTLE LIE."

*A liar will not be believed, even
when he speaks the truth.*
—Aesop

Over thirty years ago, Kip—a good friend, an attorney, and a man I deeply admire—did something he thought was in the best interests of his client: he signed his client's name to a legal contract. Here's the backstory: The Highway Patrol stopped a man traveling through Utah for speeding. The officer thought something was suspicious about the guy, so he did a quick search of the car. He found a bag with $100,000 in cash. Who carries that much cash? The officer suspected it could be payment for drugs, so he impounded the car and the cash and took the man in for questioning. The man asked for the name of a good local attorney, and someone gave him Kip's contact information.

Kip met with the man and heard his story. It appeared there was no nefarious reason he had so much cash, so Kip worked it out with the judge for the man to be released, so he could return home to California, but the court confiscated the cash until more facts could be learned.

As the case wound through the justice system, Kip got the court to release the money. He had trouble connecting with the man during these weeks, and when the papers came to actually return the cash, Kip couldn't get him on the phone. The court set a deadline for signing the release, and as the days went by, Kip still couldn't reach his client.

> **We tell lies when we are afraid ... afraid of what we don't know, afraid of what others will think, afraid of what will be found out about us. But every time we tell a lie, the thing that we fear grows stronger.—Tad Williams**

Finally, the day came. Kip was certain the man wanted his money back, so he decided to sign the document and submit it to the court. In his opinion, this was a reasonable and expedient way to move the process along.

When the man received the money, he called to set up a meeting. He drove back to Utah and walked into Kip's office. Kip handed him the money and an invoice for his services, and the man walked out the door. As he walked to his car, Kip's administrative assistant followed him. She said, "I know you're glad you got your money, but Kip signed your name on the document. I don't know if that makes you mad or not."

He instantly realized he had leverage over Kip. He sued Kip, who admitted to the court that he signed the man's name because he had told him to do whatever it required to get his money back. He didn't lie; he didn't hide what he'd done. He had tried to serve his client well, so he took a shortcut, an expedient way to do what his client had asked him to do. (After three decades, Kip still has no idea why his admin took the initiative to torpedo him and his career. It remains a mystery to him.)

Kip was convicted. My friend was branded as a felon which ruined his business and tarnished his reputation for the rest of his life. He's a wonderful man with a lovely family. Before and after that fateful day, he has walked with integrity, but that one moment, only seconds of the pen to the page, has had a devastating impact. From time to time, people who don't know him well and want to sting him bring up the incident. Maybe they're just curious, or maybe they're assholes who get a kick out of making fun of people who have screwed up. Whatever the motive, he relives the lie and the dishonor.

The Golden Rule is as simple and profound as it gets, but I think a lot of people missed that class.

Kip is one of the most wonderful and honest people I've ever known. I have always had the greatest respect for him. In this instance, he had the best of intentions, but he knew better. He thought he was serving his client well, but it came back to bite him. It was wrong of him to sign his client's name, but it's also wrong for people in the community to never forgive him. The black mark next to his name has been a stubborn stain, but over the years, he has proven himself again. We have seen his humility and his commitment to honesty, but others keep bringing up the past. If he had continued a pattern of dishonesty, I'd understand, but continuing to drive him into the ground decades after the event is, in my opinion, a character flaw at least as big.

I know people at different levels of government and business who are unscrupulous. They've cut every corner and told plenty of lies to get ahead, but they've never been caught. Some of them are Kip's fiercest critics. I want to ask them, "What if we air your dirty laundry? Would you keep yapping about my friend?" or maybe, "Aren't you glad people were kind to you when your poor judgment got you in trouble?" The Golden Rule is as simple and profound as it gets, but I think a lot of people missed that class.

Every lie is a poison; there are no harmless lies. Only the truth is safe. Only the truth gives me consolation—it is the one unbreakable diamond.—Leo Tolstoy

---

Is my friend, a convicted felon, a more despicable person than those who have done much worse but didn't get caught? Of course not. The measure of integrity isn't getting caught or not; it's doing the right thing and speaking the truth even when we're disadvantaged by our honorable actions and our honest words.

In a sense, every person in business has a fiduciary role in the lives of our clients and customers. They put their trust and their money in our hands, and they expect us to treat them with the utmost respect. We have the honor of stepping into their lives to receive some of their hard-earned money and take care of them and their families. Instead of looking for any edge to make another dollar out of the relationship, we should be grateful for their trust and the opportunity to serve them.

Can people tell if we're willing to hedge the truth for personal gain? Sometimes, but not always. I know business leaders who scammed people for years while they were respected members of the community. A friend, I'll call him Joseph (This is me, too.), was referred to a financial manager by someone he trusted. He moved all his investments to the new guy, and three years later when he called to set up an appointment, he was told the guy had been fired—for fraudulent business practices, charging exceptionally high commissions on certain products . . . including Joseph's. Should Joseph have done more homework before trusting this guy? Obviously, but the person who recommended him gave a glowing report.

The story doesn't end there. Joseph set up a meeting with the man who had taken over the account. When Joseph walked into his office, he felt like he had stepped into a mobster movie. The new guy was, as Joseph described him, "slimy." He was arrogant and slick, acting like Joseph should be honored to do business with him. In only a few minutes, Joseph realized he didn't and wouldn't ever trust this guy, so he walked out and found someone else to manage his investments.

BIG AND LITTLE

There are big lies, like fraud, and little lies, like making promises we don't keep. How many times have I heard someone say, "I'll get that information and call you right back." Yeah, right. Sometimes they do; often they don't. This line is a way to blow people off—just to get them off the phone, so we can move on to things that really matter to us. If we reflect at all on the promise, we think, *Oh, she won't even remember. I'm busy; she's busy. It's no big deal.* The underlying assumption is probably, *As long as her check clears, we're good. All that matters is the sale. If she's a bit upset, she'll get over it. I just have to hit my quota!*

When we're under pressure to produce, we're tempted to tell people whatever will make the sale or get them off our backs. So we shade the truth, we talk people into products they don't really need (or want), and when they realize what we've done, we can't back down without being exposed. Instead, we double down, upselling something else they don't need. These, my friends, are unethical business practices.

Let me ask you a question: have you ever lied? Of course you have. Admit it. Let me identify some ways you and I lie:

1) White lies

These are the most common. We say we like something we really don't, we claim we're fine with ordering pizza when we had it last night, and we claim we already knew a fact when we didn't. By far, the most common response is when people ask, "How are you?" and we reply, "Fine," even though we're dying inside.

2) Exaggeration

We want to look good, we want to impress people, so we claim our sales are bigger than they were, our fish was bigger, the crowd was bigger, and on and on. If we're skilled at this form of lying, we exaggerate just enough so people don't question us about the truth of what we're saying.

3) Minimization

We want to avoid looking bad, so we downplay mistakes and failures. We claim, "It's no big deal," when it really was.

4) Deflecting lies

Someone invites us to an event, but we don't want to go. Instead of speaking the truth (hopefully with tact), we claim, "Oh, I'd love to, but I have something going on that night. I'm so bummed that I can't go." All you had going on was binge-watching *Yellowstone*.

5) Deception

We carefully construct an alternate reality to fool a person about a product, its cost, or our intentions. This is fraud. We fudge our list of expenses, or we move sales to a different month to inflate our numbers. And offering products your company doesn't provide isn't just unfair to the customer; it's stupid.

6) Omission

Whether in a business deal or a casual conversation, we leave out important facts that would change the other person's perception. This is deception in reverse. Also, a lack of full disclosure is a form of lying.

7) Compulsive lies

Some people have lied so often that they don't even know what's true anymore. This can happen to anyone but especially addicts who have practiced telling lies for years to avoid responsibility for their substance abuse or compulsive behavior. As the saying goes, "All addicts are liars." They believe they have to lie to function around people who would hold them accountable.

8) Gaslighting

This may be the most harmful form of lying. Gaslighting is a form of psychological control that makes the victim question reality. For instance, strongly contradicting what the victim knows is true, denying an event took place even when it's plain that it did, making the victim doubt their memory, and accusing the victim of overreacting when questioning the abuser is completely valid. The effect is for the relationship to be entirely one-sided—the perp has all the power.

9) The best of intentions

Before you put all your lies in this category, let me say that very few belong here. Mark's decision to sign his client's name qualifies, but few others do. It doesn't count to lie to cover up another person's irresponsible behavior, like calling your spouse's boss to say he or she is sick when your spouse is hung over and needs detox. However, if a killer is pointing a gun at you and asking where your daughter is, by all means, lie, and lie convincingly.

At the heart of all lies is one of two driving factors: fear or pride. We're afraid of losing respect, status, safety, or something else we value, so we say whatever will protect ourselves from pain or punishment. Sometimes, we lie to protect someone we love from harm. Or we want to project an air of power and prestige, so we say whatever will impress people. We long for respect, honor, and praise, and we believe the best way to get it is to stretch the truth of our accomplishments and minimize our failures.

> *A good reputation is earned over years of treating people with respect, but we can lose that reputation in a heartbeat.*

Here's the deal: lying is a big issue. People trust us; they expect us to speak the truth to them about our products, costs, timing, and benefits. Yes, getting the sale is important, but not at the expense of our integrity. In many types of companies, there's no "meat on the bone" in serving customers after the sale. In other words, we don't make any more money for serving them well. But we lose customers (and their money) when we don't return calls, we're late to appointments, we're disorganized, and we deflect, exaggerate, or minimize. A good reputation is earned over years of treating people with respect, but we can lose that reputation in a heartbeat.

A CULTURE OF LIES

So far, I've focused on individuals shading the truth or intentionally deceiving customers or management, but it helps to take a broader view. In an article in *Harvard Business Review*, Ron Carucci reports the results of a fifteen-year study to identify factors that determine honesty within companies' management structures. He cites:

> *The stakes here are high. Accenture's Competitive Agility Index—a 7,000-company, 20-industry analysis, for the first time tangibly quantified how a decline in stakeholder trust impacts a company's financial performance. The analysis reveals more than half (54%) of companies on the index experienced a material drop in trust—from incidents such as product recalls, fraud, data breaches and c-suite*

missteps—which equates to a minimum of $180 billion in missed revenues. Worse, following a drop in trust, a company's index score drops 2 points on average, negatively impacting revenue growth by 6% and EBITDA by 10% on average.[26]

Carucci and his team identified four factors:

1) A lack of strategic clarity

   When the company's mission, vision, and values aren't clear, employees are almost three times more likely to lie or withhold information. When the top management doesn't seem to know what they're doing, morale wanes and people are more likely to cut corners.

2) Unjust accountability systems

   People thrive when they perceive they're treated fairly, but when they believe "the system" is against them, some feel justified in taking advantage or sabotaging the company.

3) Poor organizational governance

   Similarly, when employees don't believe their managers are acting with integrity, they resent pressure to perform, and rumors replace transparency. The absence of open and honest conversations demoralizes employees and makes at least some of them believe they deserve an edge.

4) Silos[27]

   Lack of good communication among the divisions of a company can create unnecessary conflict, making employees develop an "us against them" mentality. When this happens, the full range of untruths can abound: exaggerating the other side's flaws, minimizing our own, deceiving to get an advantage, and trying to make people think they're crazy.

If you're in management, creating a healthy culture isn't optional. It matters to your employees, your customers and clients, your bottom line, and your mental health. We live in a real world with flawed people, but we can construct an environment that brings out the best in them.

THE RIGHT KIND OF PRIDE

You represent a company with proven products and good (if not excellent) service. If that's not true, you need to find a job somewhere else! Make sure you work with a company whose values align with yours, so you can be proud of your association with them. When you meet with others in your industry, don't take potshots at your management. Don't run them down as a way to show what a suffering hero you are. Honor those who write your paychecks. I'm not saying you should be blind to problems in your company, but handle them in the right way by talking to people who will hear you and will consider making changes.

You're a professional with quality products. It's not a badge of honor to have the lowest price. You may be charging more because what you offer is worth more. Don't apologize for the prices of your products, your commissions, sales charges, or any other aspect of doing business. You probably don't set those prices and fees, so don't feel that you have to defend them. In my company, we offer better products, better service, better communication, better community relations, and better almost everything compared to others in our industry. My firm is price-conscious; sometimes our cost is higher than other carriers, but we're worth every penny. I won't apologize for that.

WHAT ABOUT BOB?

A few years ago, Bob changed jobs. He wanted to make more money, and he believed a commission-only role would work well for him. It didn't. He didn't realize how cutthroat the insurance industry can be, so as the months went by, he got more in debt. He assumed there would be a slow start, but he also assumed he'd make quick progress. He owed the company money for marketing resources, and his credit cards were maxed out. Desperate, one day Bob wrote a fake policy and sent it in. He hoped no one would see through his charade, and after a few days, he wrote another one. He used different names, addresses, and contract values, and he hoped no one would double-check them. He relished the idea of making some money to take the pressure off. He believed this was his only option to pay this month's rent and buy groceries for his wife and three kids. Desperation can make fools of us, and it did for Bob. His self-justification only lasted a few weeks. When the truth came out, he lost his license, ruined his reputation, embarrassed his wife, and found himself on the wrong side of the law.

Later, Bob told me, "Tyler, it was really hard to write that first phony policy. I knew I shouldn't do it, and I felt really guilty. I thought a lot about what would happen if (more likely when) I got caught, but I wrote it and sent it in. The second one was a little easier, and the third one was a breeze. By the tenth time, I'd convinced myself that 'everybody does it.' What a fool!"

IF YOU'RE A HABITUAL LIAR, CONGRATULATIONS— FAILURE IS YOUR ONLY FUTURE.

THINK ABOUT IT

1) Have you known anyone (business executive, addict, friend, etc.) whose lies got them in huge trouble? What were the consequences?
2) Review the types of lies. Which of these are easy to excuse or even defend? Which ones cause the most damage?
3) What kind of lies are the result of fear?
4) What kind is the result of pride?
5) What kind of lies are you most tempted to use? What's the purpose? How do these lies affect you and your relationships?

The numbers just don't add up. I thought things would have improved by now, but I'm bleeding money just to keep the doors open. I need to cut back on expenses as much as I can. That only makes sense. I know my office, my marketing, and my clothes can't compare with the "big shots" down the street, but I'm doing the best I can. Someday, I'll make it big, so I can afford to spend more, but not today. I have to go home each day and look at the faces of my family. How can I justify spending money on marketing when we're barely hanging on at home?

CHAPTER 8
"I CAN'T AFFORD IT."

Some people don't like change, but you need to embrace change if the alternative is disaster.
—Elon Musk

Sometimes, when I've walked into people's offices, I've wondered what a couple with several million to invest or who want to insure a lake house would think when they came through the doors. They're used to meeting with bankers, lawyers, and doctors who have fine furnishings in beautiful buildings, but that's not what I see in these other offices.

The building they've rented or bought is old. It looks like it was built before the war—the Civil War.

The person's desk looks like it came from a used furniture store—with scratches and scrapes, and it hasn't been dusted and waxed in decades.

I haven't seen a carpet like that since the 60s. I didn't think shag could last this long.

The sign outside was printed on a banner because the person didn't want to shell out a couple of thousand dollars for a sharp and permanent one.

The computer on the desk was the first one off Steve Jobs's assembly line.

You get the idea. The couple would look around and suddenly remember an appointment that conflicts with this time. They would get out of there in a flash!

Only those who dare to fail greatly, can ever achieve greatly. — Robert F. Kennedy

---

I've gone into real estate firms, insurance agencies, and all kinds of other companies whose facilities send a loud and clear message: "I'm just about broke, so I really need your business!" That's not the message you want to communicate. Your office, furniture, and ambiance need to calmly but boldly say, "I've handled big money and clients like you many times. You can trust me."

Very early in my career, I was one of those business owners who was afraid to spend any money on my office, my clothes, my car, or anything else. I maxed out all my credit cards. When I went to conferences out of town, I couldn't afford to stay in hotels, so I slept in my car. I went to the hotel restroom on the first floor each morning to wash up and shave. Every stinkin' day, I looked abject failure square in the face.

Utterly desperate for some help, I went to a conference in Iowa where Gary Kinder was speaking about managing a business through a startup. Gary was already a legend as an Olympic athlete, bestselling author, attorney, and entrepreneur. During a break, I waited my turn in line to have a minute or two with him. I hoped he'd give me the advice that would turn my career around—or more accurately, jumpstart it because the engine was already dead! As the guy in front of me shook Gary's hand and walked away, I knew this was it . . . the moment that would change everything. I was equally excited and embarrassed. Should I come clean with him and tell him the truth about my situation or ask some abstract question to save face? I had nothing to lose, so I said, "Mr. Kinder, I'm new to the insurance business, and I'm in trouble." He asked me a question or two, and I filled in a few blanks for him. The last question he asked was, "How many employees do you have?"

Didn't he understand? Couldn't he tell? I mumbled, "Well, none. I'm a one-man shop. I don't have any money. I can't do that."

Instantly, he told me, "Yes, you can. In fact, you can't afford NOT to hire a staff member. Go home and hire someone immediately." He paused for a second to let it sink in, and then he filled in a little more detail, "Don't take more than a month to hire someone."

Twenty years from now you will be more disappointed by the things you didn't do than by the ones you did. So throw off the bowlines. Sail away from the safe harbor. Catch the trade winds in your sails. Explore. Dream. Discover.—Mark Twain

---

I walked away thoroughly confused. My heart sank. There was no way I could afford to hire anybody. I couldn't even pay myself!

I had a dozen really good reasons why I couldn't follow his advice, but this was Gary Kinder. How could I claim to be smarter than him? I believed him. I trusted him. And I was desperate enough to try anything.

A few minutes later, I imagined a conversation with Tiffany: "Hey honey, I know we're in debt up to our eyeballs, and both of us are so stressed that we can't think of anything but a bleak future, but I'm going to hire someone for my business. Trust me. It'll be great!" I was pretty sure she wouldn't think it was all that great. I remembered our last big blowup: A week before, I told her I needed a new printer because the old one was so unreliable. It made perfect sense—in that day, everything was on paper, so you couldn't do business without a good printer. It cost $160, but to her, it may as well have been $10 million. She thought I'd lost my mind to buy a new printer when we couldn't afford food.

THE HIGH COST OF CHEAP

I get it. When your bank account is in the single digits, it's very hard to spend any money. In fact, the account balance screams much louder than common sense that says, "To make money, you have to spend money." That sentence seems utterly stupid . . . but it's true. Let me identify some ways being cheap is terribly expensive:

1) It affects your brand.

You don't think you can afford a professional designer, so you create your logo and signs yourself . . . and they look like they were designed by some kid in junior high. When people see it, they instantly compare your image to the others on television and down the street. Marketing and leadership expert Seth Godin notes, "A brand is the set of expectations, memories, stories and relationships that, taken together, account for the consumer's decision to choose one product or service over another."[28]

2) It tells prospective customers you're a loser.

Your brand is the story you tell in your community, and being cheap tells a loud and clear story... and people talk. Scott Cook, co-founder of Intuit, remarks, "A brand is no longer what we tell the consumer it is—it is what consumers tell each other it is."[29]

3) It tells the business community you're not a player.

Successful people know what it takes to start and run a business. When they see you cutting costs and being cheap, they quickly come to the conclusion you're not really serious about creating a great business. Referrals are the lifeblood of business, and if other professionals aren't referring people to you, you're in big trouble.

4) It marginalizes you in the community.

Reputation is everything. The perspective of potential customers and the business community can sink or float a business, and when you're too frugal, they don't pay attention to you. They may see you as pitiful, but that's worse than not noticing you.

5) It creates a devastating feedback loop.

Being cheap may seem like the wise course of action, especially when a business is starting or struggling, but it doesn't impress customers and doesn't draw referrals, so fewer people buy the products or services. The wrong response? Being even cheaper.

6) It demoralizes you.

Big visions are shattered on the hard, cold floor of cheapness, and when a vision dies, your heart withers away. You keep going through the motions for a while, but sooner or later, one of two things happens: you give up and get another job where you don't take any risks (and you don't have any dreams), or the death of your dream is just the wakeup call you've needed. You find the courage to launch your business again, but this time, with a realistic assessment of what it will take to be successful.

Business owners often believe they can cut costs by *not* hiring three kinds of professionals: attorneys, accountants, and team members. In an article in *Entrepreneur*, Carol Roth states:

> *I am a max-for-the-minimum, champagne on a beer budget kind of girl. I love to get a good deal, especially when running my business. However, while entrepreneurs know that every penny counts when running your own business, sometimes your efforts to save money can backfire, costing you more in the long run.*

She points out that getting cousin Larry, who is fresh out of law school, to handle your lawsuit may not be the smart play if saving $100 an hour costs you $100,000 when you lose your case. Hiring an accountant can make or break a company. Roth says:

> *Professional accountants do more than keep your books. The real value of accountants comes in their ability to look at rows and columns of numbers, and read them like a professor of literature would read a Shakespearean play. They don't just compute your numbers—they interpret them.*

> They can spot potential areas of financial trouble, make sure that you take all appropriate tax breaks, avoid tax penalties, identify product and service pricing issues and point out opportunities for growing your business.
>
> And hiring qualified, competent, eager staff members is essential. Those who interact with customers and vendors "are the ambassadors of your company. Saving a few dollars on untrained, unskilled people can cost you a fortune."[30]

Starting and running a business carries inherent risks. There's no getting around that fact, but the type of funding can make or break the enterprise . . . and the entrepreneur. In an article in *Inc.*, Jon Staff, founder and CEO of Getaway, says the risks aren't as great as many people assume. He describes his experience in starting two companies. He launched Getaway by raising more than $80 million from investors. That's pressure, but he experienced even more stress when he and a friend opened a frozen yogurt shop when they were in college. The only money they could get was from a bank that required a personal guarantee, which meant everything he owned was on the hook if the shop failed.

Fear is not real. The only place that fear can exist is in our thoughts of the future. It is a product of our imagination, causing us to fear things that do not at present and may not ever exist. That is near insanity. Do not misunderstand me—danger is very real, but fear is a choice. —Will Smith

---

One of the biggest and most common mistakes people make when starting a business is failing to raise enough money to start well and maintain a level of excellence until it becomes profitable. With enough capital, they can usually weather the early period and create a going concern. Staff concludes:

> Some ventures are truly risky. Mortgaging the house to expand the farm is risky. Making art is risky. Bootstrapping your startup with a house full of kids or parents to take care of is risky. Spending your life doing something you hate because it feels safer, to me, is risky. Starting a venture-backed company where you get paid a salary and have a shot at participating in an exit is not that risky.[31]

Don't get me wrong, I'm not saying don't worry about the details and just go for it. I'm saying the devil is in the details and taking an educated approach to your risk takes the guesswork out. Warren Buffett famously stated, "Risk comes from not knowing what you're doing." Do your homework, understand the risks and their consequences, then make a calculated, educated decision.

THE BIG PICTURE

The problem of being cheap isn't just about signs, desks, and antique staplers; it's about not grasping the economics of starting a business. According to a Bureau of Labor Statistics report on more than 730,000 new businesses, more than 20 percent fail in the first year and 38 percent by the third year. Very few entrepreneurs have a fat trust fund to bankroll their new ventures. The rest of us need to be prudent, for sure, but find enough capital to see us through the lean times of getting the business off the ground. Starting cheap is one of the biggest factors in the failure of new businesses.

In an article in *Inc.*, "serial business builder" Jeremy Ames describes the risks of being too cheap. He begins with his credentials: "Over the past 20 years, I've had a front-row seat for the launch of more than 30,000 small businesses. Some clear patterns emerge when looking at the differences between those that succeeded and those that failed." Among the common mistakes, he identifies:

1) Failure to do enough market research

We've all heard the story of the marketing meeting at the company selling dog food. People sit around talking about why sales are so low, offering many different takes on the problem, and then someone says, "The dogs don't like it!" Some people start businesses because they've had a dream of making it big, but it was all lollipops and unicorns. They didn't do the hard work to understand the need for their product or service, gauge the competition, and, with clear-eyed reasoning, determine if starting the business is even feasible in that community and economic climate. They pour what little money they have into a bottomless pit.

2) Lack of a workable financial model

Ames comments, "I'm continually shocked by how many entrepreneurs willingly spend thousands of dollars to launch a new business without a budget or cash flow projection. Building a financial model forces you to identify the key assumptions that drive the financial success of a business." Some of us are nerds and love to work on spreadsheets, but many entrepreneurs assume they can be successful because of their winning personality. (See how that works for you!)

3) Insufficient capital

Assumptions. A big vision can lead to a huge collapse if the new business doesn't have enough capital to get traction. Ames suggests you estimate how long it will take to become profitable, and then double the length of time. That's more realistic.

4) Too much debt[32]

This is the ugly twin sister of not having enough capital. Sure, borrowing money creates debt, but not borrowing enough money puts you underwater really fast. When banks and other lenders don't see enough progress, they first talk to you like you crashed your bike into your dad's car; then they talk to you like you stole his car!

If you're thinking about starting a business, find a professional coach or mentor who will do his best to talk you out of it. If, after being thoroughly grilled about every conceivable risk, you decide to move forward, you'll at least have your eyes open. If you're in the middle of a startup and things aren't progressing as fast as you hoped, a coach or mentor can give you a hardnosed assessment of where you are and what it will take to be successful. No more shortcuts, no more fairyland assumptions. (Kill all the unicorns!) Being realistic will help you sleep at night, you won't bark at your spouse and kids (as much), and you just might become a real success in business.

REVERSIBLE DAMAGE

I have a young friend in another state (I'll call him Brett) who called me several times during his first year in business, and I was glad to offer any benefits of my experience. I could tell he wasn't hitting it out of the park, but I had no idea it had been such a struggle. When I saw Brett at an agency meeting, he looked like he'd been dragged a mile through scrub brush. I've been around long enough to recognize that Brett was suffering financially and emotionally, and he was mentally fatigued. I invited him and his wife, Jaclyn, to spend a day with me in my office. I discussed their situation with my wife, Tiffany, and we knew we had to intervene. After all, I had been where they currently were. When I was starting out, plenty of people had the ability to help, but they looked right through me as if I was already gone from the business and a distant memory. At the time, I desperately needed a mentor and friend, but as I looked around, all I could see were others living the high life, and I was jealous as hell. Now, with Brett and Jaclyn, this was my chance to make a difference in someone's life, and I couldn't wait to help this young couple.

Just before they arrived, I had flashbacks of my struggles when I was starting out. I had felt anxious, afraid, and desperate, and I was sure Brett and Jaclyn were rowing in the same boat now.

They pulled up in an old-model car that barely got them there with their infant in the back seat. They came in with total despair on their faces. I suspected they didn't even have gas money to drive the three hours home after we met, but they were desperate, so they came. You could have been blind and still felt their body language screaming that, frankly, life sucked. Tiffany and I sat across from them in a private conference room. We were full of understanding and love for these dear people. I began by asking Jaclyn, "Tell me. How has your first year in business been for you?"

I was determined to help them turn around the powerful tide of failure.

Instantly, all the tears she had been holding in for months started flowing. This wasn't a calm cry. Tiffany, seeing what discerning women see, got up and sat next to Jaclyn and hugged her for a long time. She cried for the next twenty minutes.

I looked at Brett; he, too, had broken into tears, and so did Tiffany and I. Between sobs, Jaclyn told me about the horrors of the year: they'd maxed out their credit cards after only a few months, and they were barely making enough for food and gas. They even had to borrow rent money from her mother. For them, it was a humiliating experience. We were blessed to meet them on a very personal level, and we gave them every ounce of understanding and compassion in us. As we talked and cried, I realized that years before, I had needed the kind of care Tiffany and I were giving this couple. I was determined to help them turn around the powerful tide of failure.

Starting a business is an exercise in tremendous hope, and if it goes south, people can find themselves in a very dark place. Brett's confidence was shot, his marriage was struggling, and he had lost hope in his future. Failure created a death spiral into a black hole that consumed everything good.

I appreciate Brett's heart, but I got the long end of the stick in this relationship.

I took them under my wing, gave them some seed money, and offered to mentor Brett, and things began to turn around. I've thought about him many times since that tearful day at the conference. I've thought, *I wish someone would have done for me what I was able to do for him. It would have made a huge difference!* Brett and I talked every week for a year and a half. My goal wasn't just to help him get out of financial bondage; I wanted him to regain his confidence, restore his relationship with his wife, have a positive attitude when meeting with prospective clients, and begin to believe in his future again. Thankfully, Brett was open to my coaching, and he's now a successful, hopeful guy. But that's not all—he's also one of the most compassionate people I know. He identifies with those who are at the bottom or are headed in that direction, and he's paying forward the love and attention I've given him.

Twenty years from now you will be more disappointed by the things you didn't do than by the ones you did. So throw off the bowlines. Sail away from the safe harbor. Catch the trade winds in your sails. Explore. Dream. Discover.—Mark Twain

---

Not long ago, Brett called, not to ask a question or get advice. He said, "Tyler, you saved my career, you saved my marriage, and I don't think it's too much to say that you saved my life. I'm beyond grateful." I appreciate Brett's heart, but I got the long end of the stick in this relationship. I've had the joy of seeing the little bit of wisdom I've gained over a lifetime used to change his life.

He's grateful for me, and I'm equally (or more) grateful for him reaching out to me.

Did it cost me some time? Yes, but it paid off far more than it cost.

Did it keep me sharp? Yes, because I had to go back and think through why I do everything I do.

Did the involvement deplete my reservoir of energy? Not in the least. It gave me more passion for multiplying myself in the lives of people like Brett.

Did it reinforce my sense of purpose? Oh, yes, more than you can imagine.

Are you in Brett's shoes? Find a kind and wise mentor.

Are you in my shoes? Pour your life into someone like Brett.

This is the easiest close of a chapter ever:

IF YOU WON'T (NOT CAN'T, BUT WON'T) FIND A WAY TO RUN YOUR BUSINESS PROPERLY AND WISELY, THEN CONWGRATULATIONS—YOUR FINANCIAL FAILURE IS CLOSER THAN YOU THINK.

THINK ABOUT IT

1) Do you know anyone in business who has a reputation for being cheap? If you do, how has that reputation affected the person and the business?
2) Has there been a time when you didn't make enough to live on? How did you respond to this dilemma?
3) Look back at "The High Cost of Cheap." Which of the consequences seems most devastating to you? Explain your answer.
4) Are you tempted to look for a "bargain basement" attorney, accountant, and team members? Why or why not?
5) Do you need to make any changes in the way you view the investment in your business? If so, what are they?

Self-absorbed? Who are you kidding? This is just the way life works. I'm happy when you win, but only if I have bigger wins. I'm not in this for you. I'm in it for me. The one who dies with the biggest boat, the biggest bank account, the biggest house, and the finest car wins . . . and I'm determined to be that person. Don't like it? Tough. I don't care what you think, and I certainly don't want to hear your opinions about my choices in life. You, like everyone else, are dumber than a box of rocks, so get off my case!

CHAPTER 9
"IT'S ALL ABOUT ME."

Seek first to understand, then to be understood.
—Steven Covey

As I prepared to write this chapter, I had a fascinating experience. I went to the post office to pick up my mail (yes, I still do that), and on my way out, a lady decided this was it ... *this* was the day she would tell the world about how incredibly smart and talented her kids and grandkids are! And man, she didn't hold back. Her self-adulation was primarily directed toward the clerk, who was a captive audience behind the counter, but I just couldn't walk away because it was a social experiment we were watching in real-time. I wanted to see the end of this drama! She raved mostly about her kids and grandkids. She talked about them as if they had just saved civilization with their wit and their abundance of talent.

Her boasts were a spectacle for the ages. Her grandchildren were obviously a gift from the heavens (or maybe only in the nether world of her mind) for their brilliance and skill. Finally, she exhausted the limits of her pride.

I enjoyed it immensely; I'm not going to lie. She was so happy when she left. She nodded to both of us, lifted her head a bit like she was the Queen of Sheba, and walked away. The clerk and I looked at each other, but we didn't say a word. We didn't need to because we each knew exactly what the other was thinking. We smiled at each other and chuckled, and I walked out. Please don't assume that I was laughing at her. I absolutely was not. I loved the experience and was grateful to be there when she needed to vent to someone.

Lead by listening—to be a good leader you have to be a great listener.—Richard Branson

---

When I got in my car, I couldn't stop thinking about this encounter. I was sure she thought she'd had a wonderful conversation with us, even though all we did was punctuate her unending self-adulation with: "Wow," "That's amazing," "Really cool," and "Good for you." I realized she hadn't taken a breath for ten minutes to let the clerk and me say more than a couple of words, and all she wanted was an audience, not a conversation. She needed validation by feeling heard. I was totally glad to be there for her.

As I drove to my appointment, I thought about this chance encounter, and I went back over how body language communicated loudly and clearly. Not just the lady, but the clerk and me too. Especially me. Then it hit me . . . I do the same thing! Not all the time, but far too often. My mind flashed back to some recent meetings when I was thinking, *Holy cow! How many more stories about your kids do I have to endure? I'm glad you gave birth to the smartest, most athletic, and most talented children ever to grace the planet, but enough! Yes, I agree, they're certainly going to Harvard or MIT—or maybe both! One is going to be president, and the other will cure cancer, but I'm so tired of you yapping that my brain is going numb. Somebody, please shoot me!*

It's hard to admit that I'm not really interested in people 100 percent of the time, but it happens. When I feel pressured and have a million things to do, I have a sense of urgency. I want to be efficient, so I don't have time to hear all the *blah de blah*. I need to move to the next project . . . stat! Idle chatter isn't what I need at the moment. If they want to talk about their families or ask the same question three different ways, I become impatient and look for an opening to say, "Anything else?" which is not-so-subtle code for, "I'm done. How about you?" I'm really glad they don't say, "Hey, Tyler, are you paying attention? Do you even care?" I would be mortified if that happened, but I wouldn't blame them. It may be human nature to be self-absorbed, but it's *flawed* human nature.

That day in the post office, I saw patience in action. The clerk didn't act impatient in the least. She gave eye contact, leaned forward, and gestured that she was really interested. I don't know if it was an Oscar-worthy performance or the real thing, but she gets my vote for treating that lady with the utmost respect.

Can you imagine going to work and having the people around you in the office and your customers believe in the depths of their souls that you truly care for them? I believe that if enough of us did that, it would change the world . . . or at least our corner of it.

LISTEN, REALLY LISTEN

How can I tell if someone is really listening to me? I'll list a few important elements in a minute, but I'll begin with the clearest indication someone is "tracking with me": it's when they ask a second and third question. We live in a fast-paced, transactional world. We want to give and get answers (preferably the right ones) immediately. No waiting. No beating around the bush. "Just the facts, ma'am. Just the facts." People ask me questions all day every day. Sometimes, all they want are factoids about an insurance policy or an investment vehicle. I get into the mode of being "the answer man." "Just come to me, and I'll tell you what you want to know." But some people want more than facts. They want my opinion about something they care about, and sometimes, they want more than that—they want my friendship. When I give short, crisp answers to these questions, many of them know I'm "in the zone" (the transactional zone), and they want more, so they ask a second question, maybe about my family, my views on an important social matter, my faith, or something completely different. Too often, I'm so dense that I stay in my transactional zone and give a clipped answer. If they're exceedingly patient with me, they smile and say something like, "Tyler, I really want you to tell me what you're thinking and feeling about this."

Attentive listening to others lets them know that you love them and builds trust, the foundation of a loving relationship.—Brian Tracy

---

Thinking. Got it. Feeling? Not so much. People who ask second and third questions care about me, not just what I know. They want to enter my world and rummage around a bit, getting past my relational resistance and fact-obsessed mind. Actually, that's where I want to live, too, so when I finally realize that's what they're doing, I'm all in!

Now that I've made my main point, here's one that's in second place. I've learned that one statement is "conversation gold": "Tell me more about that."

So... what about me? How often do I engage people beyond fact-based transactions to get to know them a little more? How many times do I ask the second and third questions?

Now that I've made my main point, here's one that's in second place. I've learned that one statement is "conversation gold": "Tell me more about that." It's a type of second question, and it's immensely flexible. You can say it to almost anyone who's describing a situation. Even if you believe you have enough facts, say it anyway. You may uncover some gems that would have remained hidden if you hadn't asked for more.

In an article in *Harvard Business Review*, Robin and Boris Groysberg report that almost four out of five business schools say "presenting" is a learning goal, but only about one in ten say "listening" is as important. They explain:

> A participant in any conversation has two goals: first, to understand what the other person is communicating (both the overt meaning and the emotion behind it) and second,

to convey interest, engagement, and caring to the other person. This second goal is not "merely" for the sake of kindness, which would be reason enough. If people do not feel listened to, they will cease to share information.

When people talk, listen completely. Most people never listen.—Ernest Hemingway

---

Good listeners combine information, emotion, and action.[33] They don't settle for "just the facts." They explore to find out more, asking second and third questions and saying, "Tell me more about that." They're aware of their emotions during the conversation so they can overcome their boredom and manage any anger or anxiety. They're also aware of the other person's emotions so they can back off a bit or wade in more deeply, whichever is warranted. Their actions during and after the interaction communicate that they're fully engaged, leaning in (but not too far), sitting up (but not standing up), and speaking clearly (without fierceness or timidity).

So, you see, it's much more than just the facts.

DO THIS, DON'T DO THAT

I've made enough mistakes in conversations to float a boat, but I've learned a thing or two along the way. Here are my top suggestions:

1) Prepare. Don't just dive in unless it's an impromptu interaction. Many of our conversations with family, colleagues, clients, and customers are scheduled, even if the heads-up is just a minute before. A little planning can avert a world of problems: What

do I want to say? How do I want to say it? What outcome am I looking for? What potholes do I need to watch out for?

2) Start well. Don't assume you already know what's going on.

We all know that first impressions are crucial, and that's true in important conversations even with people we've known for years. If you anticipate any tension, write and memorize your opening statement, so your brain doesn't turn to mush in the first moment.

3) Watch as much as you listen. Don't be oblivious to obvious signs.

Yes, the other person's words are important, but nonverbal messages are vital too. Sometimes, body language and facial expressions perfectly parallel the words, but sometimes, they tell a different story. I've talked to plenty of people who insisted, "I'm fine," but their clenched teeth, grimaces, and closed fists sent a different message!

4) Watch yourself. Be aware of your emotions and nonverbal signals.

From time to time in the talk, take stock of yourself. In tense situations, people often resort to one of the coping strategies: fight, flight, or freeze. Are you looking to score points and win at all costs? Are you looking for the nearest exit? Are you like a deer in the headlights and can't think of what you wanted to say? When you become aware of reactions like this, you can do something about it. Otherwise, you'll just double down on your self-destructive strategy . . . and then you'll beat yourself to a pulp after the conversation is over.

5) Mirror what the person says. Don't just blast through your agenda.

This can certainly be overdone, but in detailed and emotional conversations, it's smart to stop and say, "Let me try to say what I think you're saying." You may find out you're right on target, which affirms the person and assures that you're really listening, or you may find out you've missed it. In that case, you should say, "I'm sorry. Please tell me again. Maybe this time I'll get it."

6) Stay focused. Don't drift off, and don't ignore the person while you're preparing your next statement.

It's one of the cardinal sins of communication that when the other person is talking, our minds are focused on our next witty or point-shattering response. We're not smart enough to listen well and think about our next statement at the same time. But the problem may not be thinking . . . it's the lack of thinking. I've been in conversations when minutes went by, and I had no clue what the person had said. I try to cover by nodding, mmmm-ing, and saying something incredibly witty like, "Is that right?" or "Oh, yeah."

7) Ask for feedback. Don't make it a one-way thing.

When you're in tune with the other person, you can sense if you're connecting. In one sense, this is the opposite of mirroring. Instead of saying, "Here's what I hear you saying," you're saying, "Tell me what you think of our conversation so far. Are we on the same page?" And listen. Really listen.

8) End well. Don't leave tension hanging, at least, not for long.

Part of your preparation is deciding ahead of time what you hope the outcome will be. It might be that the person leaves deeply encouraged, clearly directed, or perhaps solemnly corrected. Ending well doesn't mean the other person is thrilled with the outcome, only that you accomplished what you intended.

Abrahams and Groysberg conclude:

Now is the time for leaders to really listen, understand the context, resist the temptation to respond with generic answers, and recognize your own listening limitations—and improve on them. Have compassion for yourself—you can't scream at your own brain like a drill sergeant and whip that raw grey matter into shape. What you can do is recognize your weak points and make the necessary adjustments.[34]

Can you imagine going to work and having those around you believe in the depths of their souls that you care for them and their families and that you want the best for them? It would be a culture where people thrive, others clamor to work there, and clients flock to you because they sense genuine respect and affirmation. Isn't that what you want? Sure, it is.

Find out what moves people, what they daydream about, and what haunts their dreams at night.

How do you get there? This book (and countless others) offers hundreds of insights and tips, but I believe one is more important than them all: learn to listen. Listen well. Listen intently. Listen with a heart to understand the person not just the facts. Ask questions, then ask more questions, and ask better questions to let people know you care. Be a people person first to last. Yes, technology and statistics are important, but only because they help us serve people well. Long for your own success, but long as much for the success of those in your office and your customers. Don't settle for transactional relationships. Find out what moves people, what they daydream about, and what haunts their dreams at night. Devote yourself to doing your part to fulfill their purpose in life. If they know you're on board with that, you'll win true friends.

> **You cannot truly listen to anyone and do anything else at the same time.—M. Scott Peck**

Listen to people at your home office (or, if you're on a staff team, your employer). Some people automatically see those above them as threats. They have "a problem with authority," so they assume the worst of "those people" who "don't give a rip about us!" If this evaluation is true for you, you need to meet it head-on with good communication skills, but I've found that many of my negative assumptions about "those people" aren't true, or are at least way overblown. I need to engage instead of assuming the worst and listen instead of accusing. (And if the person remains a butthead, at least I know that's the truth!)

One of the most important lessons I've learned is to listen to people in the community—those in power and those at the other end of the power scale. I can get so wrapped up in my business, my career, and my income that I miss opportunities to get to know people who live around me. Everywhere I turn, I see people who need support, sometimes money, often some time and energy, but always a shot of compassion. Investing my time to get to know and listen to people in government, social organizations, and outreaches stretches my world to encompass far more than my little insurance business. I've gotten to know some incredible people. Troy Korsgaden has taught me a great deal about kindness and communication. Who am I to such a titan in the insurance and public speaking worlds? I don't know, but I can tell you this: when I email him, he answers, and when I need a few minutes, he gives them to me. He has written a master class in communication in his book *Discussion Partners*. He and Michelle Hubert of Korsgaden International are invested in me. I'm humbled that they care so deeply about me and my business. I can feel it, and I like it . . . a lot. I, in turn (and you, in turn), need to follow Troy's example and give ourselves to make society better than we found it.

Of course, this goes for your family, too. Don't rush by them to be warm and tender with your staff and customers! Look them in the eye, ask them second and third questions, and engage them at every level: facts, emotions, and actions.

Taking care of others and assisting them in fulfilling their dreams creates true satisfaction but be sure to allow them to progress at their own speed.

IF YOU'VE BECOME A "ME MONSTER," YOU'RE AN ASSHOLE, AND CONGRATULATIONS— YOU'RE ALREADY A FAILURE.

THINK ABOUT IT

1) When was the last (or most memorable) conversation you've had with someone who just wanted an audience? How did you feel during and after the encounter?

2) Who do you know who listens really well? What does that person do that communicates interest and engagement so powerfully?

3) What does asking second and third questions communicate to someone?

4) In what way is "Tell me more about that" conversation gold?

5) Okay, time for a test. Give yourself a score of 0 (not even a blip) to 10 (utterly amazing!) on these elements of being a great listener:

_____Prepare. Don't just dive in unless it's an impromptu interaction.

_____Start well. Don't assume you already know what's going on.

_____Watch as much as you listen. Don't be oblivious to obvious signs.

_____Watch yourself. Be aware of your emotions and non-verbal signals.

_____Mirror what the person says. Don't just blast through your agenda.

_____Stay focused. Don't drift off, and don't ignore the person while you're preparing your next statement.

_____Ask for feedback. Don't make it a one-way thing.

_____End well. Don't leave tension hanging, at least, not for long.

_____Total

What's your total score? Sixty to 80 indicates that you're a very good listener. Forty to 60 means you do some things well, but you could improve. Less than 40 shows that you need to make listening skills one of your main goals for the near future.

CHAPTER 10
"IF ONLY..."

The happiest people are those who do the most for others. The most miserable are those who do the least.
—Booker T. Washington

A few years ago, Tiffany and I had the opportunity to travel to Mali, a landlocked country in West Africa south of Algeria. It was genuinely a life-changing experience. The vast majority of the people we met were poorer than the poorest people in America. The average monthly salary is $100 to $400, with nearly half living in what the UN calls "extreme poverty." But they're far happier than most of the people I meet in the United States. The only hotel was at the United States Embassy. When we were invited to their villages and visited their villages, there was no table, no chairs, no knives, forks, or spoons... just a pot of rice, sometimes flavored with pepper. They sat on their haunches as they passed the bowl around with big smiles. We quickly noticed they ate with only their right hands because their left hands were their version of reusable toilet paper. To even go to that country, we had to have a barrage of vaccinations, and for the entire ten-day trip, we packed every bit of our food in a backpack. The people were so kind to invite us to eat with them, but we followed the strong recommendations not to for the sake of our health.

> *Life doesn't get easier or more forgiving, we get stronger and more resilient. — Steve Maraboli*

Muslim men get to have up to four wives, but Christian men are limited to two. (I thought it was discrimination against the Christian men, but Tiffany didn't see the humor in my remark.) It seemed that every woman of childbearing age was either pregnant or had a newborn. Most of the women held one or two children and led another couple of them by the hand. One day, I realized I hadn't heard a child cry since we'd been there, even though we were surrounded by kids of all ages.

We were piled into a 1960s bus of some kind with no air conditioning, and most of the seats weren't bolted down. It was 109 degrees the week we were there, and after a day or two, I wondered if I was tough enough to handle it. When we got thirsty, all we could reach for was a bottle of water that was almost as hot as the air temperature.

Day after day, encounter after encounter, I was amazed. How could these people who had so little be so content and happy? I realized they weren't anxious about climbing the corporate ladder because there is no ladder, and they aren't proud or despairing about competing with others over wealth and possessions because no one has wealth or possessions. They don't struggle with debt because no one has enough money to borrow from. They get up every day and look for ways to get enough food for themselves and their families. If they earn a little money to buy food or hunt and get some, they survive another day. If a family doesn't have enough today but someone else has a little extra, they share. As communities, they take care of the elderly, the young, the sick, and the disabled.

No one in Utah is as poor as most of the people we met in Mali. That hot African sun mercilessly beat down. A ballcap, sunglasses, and shoes were like a dream come true for them. They offered us anything they had to show appreciation for the water well the men were digging and the medical assistance Tiffany was providing. We built a "hospital" out of concrete about 12 x 12 feet and plumbed in water. There was a filing cabinet partially full of gauze, extra eyeglasses, scissors, and toothbrushes; we didn't leave any medications because they had no idea how to utilize them. We provided a gurney for a hospital bed, and the next day, an amazing young woman gave birth on the gurney. They were ecstatic to have such a nice facility for the birth of a child.

It struck me that I'm not as consistently happy because I'm often looking over my shoulder to see who's going to pass me in the race to bigger and more, and I'm often looking ahead to see if I can pass the one in front of me. When a friend attended a national conference, most of the people he met led with their name and the size of their business. They were staking out their position on the pecking order, hoping and praying they'd be ahead of most people.

COMPARISON KILLS

Comparison can have a positive effect if it inspires us to be more and do more because we want our lives to count, but too often, the motive is a bit less noble: we want to overcome our sense of inadequacy by being *more than* and *better than*. This makes us more self-absorbed, not less, and we experience envy, jealousy, increased stress, and anxiety. Even when we conquer the competition, the rush doesn't last long. Soon, we realize others are catching up, and we sure don't want to fall behind! We redouble our efforts to stay one step ahead (or convince ourselves that we can be one step ahead) of the competition. Before long, even our greatest successes feel empty and worthless. Author C. S. Lewis had clear insights about the nature of comparison:

> *Pride gets no pleasure out of having something, only out of having more of it than the next man. We say that people are proud of being rich, or clever, or good-looking, but they are not. They are proud of being richer, or cleverer, or better-looking than others. If everyone else became equally rich, or clever, or good-looking there would be nothing to be proud about. It is the comparison that makes you proud: the pleasure of being above the rest. Once the element of competition has gone, pride has gone. That is why I say that Pride is essentially competitive in a way the other vices are not.*[35]

Our culture creates and inflames discontent. In a Kenyon College commencement address, novelist David Foster Wallace looked deep into the heart of humanity and warned the graduates and their families:

> *If you worship money and things—if they are where you tap real meaning in life—then you will never have enough. Never feel you have enough. It's the truth. Worship your*

own body and beauty and sexual allure and you will always feel ugly, and when time and age start showing, you will die a million deaths before they finally plant you. On one level, we all know this stuff already—it's been codified as myths, proverbs, clichés, bromides, epigrams, parables: the skeleton of every great story. The trick is keeping the truth up front in daily consciousness. Worship power—you will feel weak and afraid, and you will need ever more power over others to keep the fear at bay. Worship your intellect, being seen as smart—you will end up feeling stupid, a fraud, always on the verge of being found out.[36]

The major value in life is not what you get. The major value of life is what you become. —Jim Rohn

---

It's interesting that Wallace described our compulsive pursuit of money, good looks, sexual pleasure, and intelligence as "worship." Was that an overstatement? I don't think so. It means we consider something *worthy*. When people worship, they're recommitting their lives to something or someone, pledging their allegiance and loyalty. Is that what we see in those who are driven to have more money, better stuff, more power, and look smarter than anyone else? Sure it is. And it's a fool's game.

I'm not saying it's wrong to have money, look handsome or pretty, enjoy sex, and be smart, but it's soul-crushing to make those things the ultimate measure of who we are. These pursuits promise fulfillment—and to be honest, they do give us satisfaction . . . until we realize someone else has a little bit more than us.

I know a lot about the destructive effects of comparison because I've fought on that battlefield for way too long. I remember that when I was starting out in business, a friend told me he was thrilled that he'd made $6,000 that month . . . gross. I replied, "That's amazing! I hope I can get there soon." I had powerful but mixed emotions. I felt ashamed that my friend was doing so much better than me, but I was fiercely driven to catch up. Looking back, isn't that funny? Six thousand gross? Starting was rough . . . really rough.

At any given moment, I can feel "more than" or "less than," and it only takes seconds to flip-flop between the two.

Today, I have to take in quite a gob of money just to keep the doors open. By all accounts, my business is doing well, but I live with the constant knowledge that others are watching me to see if I'll keep standing or if I'll fall. I've been dumbfounded by people who have told me that I have a target on my back—within my own company and region. They insisted their only goal was to beat me this year. I was shocked. I still dread hearing someone ask, "Tyler, what's going on? Why is your business slipping? What are you doing wrong?" Every rung up the ladder of success is satisfying, but it comes with higher expectations. I don't compare myself today with my friend when we were starting out. I compare myself with top producers . . . and I either feel pride if I'm keeping up with them or dread if I'm not. At any given moment, I can feel "more than" or "less than," and it only takes seconds to flip-flop between the two. That's no way to live!

What do we compare? You name it!

- Our physiques
- Our clothes
- Our spouse
- Our bank accounts
- Our homes
- Our cars
- Our children's success in school and sports
- Our vacations
- Our choice of careers
- And anything else anyone values.

A friend told me about a conversation she had with a woman at her church. My friend noticed that the woman always sat in the front row. When she asked if she felt more comfortable up front, the woman replied, "Yes, but not in the way you think. If I sit anywhere else, I spend the whole service comparing my hair, my clothes, and my figure to every woman in front of me."

Okay, here goes. I'm gonna meddle: social media is one of the chief villains in the comparison race. People post the most thrilling victories, the most beautiful and delicious meals, and the best times of their lives. When we look at them, we can't help but compare! We think, *My day was dull, but it wasn't a disaster like yesterday. Last night's dinner was a good, solid meh. And I'm so darn busy going to meetings and hauling kids to practices that I can't remember the last* peaceful time, much less the best time. If you're not brave enough to delete the apps, at least limit your exposure... and when you scroll through, notice what happens in your mind and heart. (Then you might delete them!)

SOMETHING TO LIVE FOR

Is there a solution? Should we all just retire at thirty-five and be homeless? No, ambition is neutral—it depends on what we're ambitious to achieve. We need to find something bigger than our wallets and reputations to live for. "Like what?" you want to bark at me. Okay, I'll answer that question boldly: "I don't know." I can't tell you what stirs your heart. I can't tell you what captures your imagination. I can only tell you that you won't find real fulfillment until you peel back the layers of your experience and desires to uncover "that thing" that gives you two things you can't thrive without: identity and energy.

We instinctively want to know that our lives count, that we matter, and that when we're gone, we've left at least a small dent (a positive one) in the lives of a few people. Finding a compelling purpose inevitably demands some hard choices. We won't have as much time for our other pleasures, and we'll invest money in achieving that purpose, but the payoffs are more than worth it. We'll live with the deep, soul-nourishing satisfaction that we've made a difference.

Some people move to the farthest reaches of civilization to care for the poor. It's a noble cause, but you don't have to do that.

Some people start nonprofits to touch the lives of the homeless or promote education. That's wonderful, but you don't have to do that.

Many people find (or stumble upon) an organization doing things in the community that somehow combines their time-tested talents with their desire to help the people the organization serves.

And some people devote themselves to one person, someone who is chronically sick or disabled, and pouring love into that person gives them all the meaning they need.

I can tell you one thing that truly makes me sad is wasted talent. It seems like in every industry there is a coffee shop crew or group of retirees who retired so that they can do nothing at all. Ever. Wow! I'm glad they can relax; they probably earned it. But this is a distinct group of people who have given decades of years to learning skills and talents that are so needed, and yet they sit. Talking about having what it takes to solve the world's problems but being unwilling to make the effort to actually do it. If you have retired, use your lifetime of wisdom to create a better community. Please. You are desperately needed.

EVEN A LITTLE

Don't get me wrong. I'm not asking you to leave your job and take a full-time unpaid position at a charity. (I certainly haven't done that.) But I'm asking you to take stock of how you want your life to count and what legacy you want to leave, and then find a place to dive in. If that one doesn't float your boat. No problem. Find another one.

If you're consumed by the comparison game, RELAX.

The problem of living a drab, gray, meaningless life is rampant in our culture. Leadership expert Dr. Margie Warrell cites a Gallop employee engagement survey that found "that a large majority of people go to work each day pushed along more by inertia than inspiration. In a recent study in the UK, over 90% of respondents reported that they're often just going through the motions, as though on auto-pilot, feeling anything from mildly disinterested to outright disillusioned by how they're spending the best hours of their days and best years of their lives."

Every problem is a gift—without problems, we would not grow.—Anthony Robbins

---

Before you complain, "I know. That's how I live, but I don't have a choice!" I want to assure you that yes, you have choices. You can play it safe, pursue what everyone else values, play the comparison game, and feel empty much of the time... or you can do some serious self-evaluation, search your past to identify times when you felt you were making a difference, and tailor your future to make it an integral part of your life. The journey isn't always easy. Dr. Warrell remarks:

> We all arrive at moments in our life where we are torn between retreating to the safety of the known and the possibilities of the unknown—between comfort and contribution; between security and service; between seeking admiration and *looking good* and risking status and *doing good*. Between love and fear.

We don't need to look very far to see that the psychological tug toward consolidating power, protecting pride and safeguarding status often wins. Yet it begs the question: At what cost to the state of our heart? And at what cost to the hearts of those whom we might otherwise serve?[37]

If you're consumed by the comparison game, RELAX. Take a step back and a deep breath. The mental fatigue of it all will send you to an early grave. There's always someone smarter, wealthier, funnier, and better-looking than you.

YOUR CHOICE

Please be assured that my only goal in writing this book is to help you avoid the cardinal sins associated with failure in business and your personal life. If you've been paying attention as you've read these chapters, you've recognized this entire book is really about taking care of those around you. If you haven't caught on to that so far, then know it now. This world is NOT all about you. Most of us don't even realize we've gotten caught up in that way of thinking, but I have, and so have you. We're fulfilled not by what we receive but by what we give—and primarily, giving ourselves.

If you're in management, you have the sacred role of lifting people up and helping them become more than they can be on their own. Remember, when you make a big decision, it impacts the personal lives of those you manage, sometimes in a life-altering way. Honor them by holding yourself to a higher standard—not the same standard, but a higher standard. Treat them with dignity, act with integrity, and show the same basic kindness you appreciate when others show it to you.

Will you fail in business? Yes, in many ways and many times, but you can learn and grow from each one. It's your choice. Don't waste your failures.

IF YOU INSIST ON PLAYING THE STUPID COMPARISON GAME, THEN CONGRATULATIONS—YOU'LL FIND FAILURE AT EVERY TURN.

THINK ABOUT IT

1) How would you describe the positive effects of comparison? What has to happen to the person's perspective to make comparison positive?
2) How would you describe the ways comparison kills?
3) Do you think Wallace's word "worship" accurately depicts the ways people are devoted to being smarter, wealthier, stronger, and more good-looking than others? Why or why not?
4) What makes you feel "more than" and "less than"?
5) Describe a time in your life when you had your most compelling sense of purpose. What was it? What about it was so meaningful?
6) What steps do you need to take to clarify and amplify your purpose?
7) What's the most important thing you've gotten from this book? What are you going to do about it?

ENDNOTES

1   "10 of the Most Compelling Stats from Microsoft's 'Global State of Customer Service' Report," Microsoft Dynamics 365 Community, 2 Apr 2021, https://community.dynamics.com/blogs/post/?postid=95543fd1-c6a9-4170-9f8b-ece3dc41634d.

2   Snigdha Patel, "15 Examples of Bad Customer Service & Ways to Fix Them," WalkerInfo, cited on Reve Chat, updated 21 Apr 2024, https://www.revechat.com/blog/bad-customer-service/.

3   Lance Bettencourt, "How Customers Become the Worst Enemies or the Best Friends," American Marketing Association, 4 Oct 2017, https://www.ama.org/2017/10/04/how-customers-become-the-worst-enemies-or-the-best-friends/.

4   Dennis Jaffe, "The Essential Importance of Trust: How to Build It or Restore It," Forbes, 5 Dec 2018, https://www.forbes.com/sites/dennisjaffe/2018/12/05/the-essential-importance-of-trust-how-to-build-it-or-restore-it/?sh=4288cdbd64fe.

5   Donald Sull and Charles Sull, "How to Fix a Toxic Culture," 8 Sept 2022, MIT Sloan Management Review, https://sloanreview.mit.edu/article/how-to-fix-a-toxic-culture/.

6   Levi King, "Vision Leaks and How to Repair Them," Entrepreneur, 20 July 2016, https://www.entrepreneur.com/article/275474.

7   Simon Sinek, X post, July 14, 2023, 11:39 am, https://x.com/simonsinek/status/1679878416651223043.

8   Jim Collins, "Level 5 Leadership," Jim Collins, https://www.jimcollins.com/concepts/level-five-leadership.html.

9   Erin Hutchinson, "Meaning through Mentorship: The Value of the Professional Role Model," Forbes, 15 Apr 2022, https://www.forbes.com/sites/forbescommunicationscouncil/2022/04/15/meaning-through-mentorship-the-value-of-the-professional-role-model/?sh=78212de45f57.

10   Rasmus Hougaard and Jacqueline Carter, "Ego Is the Enemy of Good Leadership," Harvard Business Review, 6 Nov 2018, https://hbr.org/2018/11/ego-is-the-enemy-of-good-leadership?registration=success.

11   Heidi Lynne Kurter, "Is Micromanaging a Form of Bullying? Here Are 3 Things You Should Know," Forbes, 29 June 2021, https://www.forbes.com/sites/heidilynnekurter/2021/06/29/is-micromanaging-a-form-of-bullying-here-are-3-things-you-should-know/?sh=752e88bc4467.

12   John Hall, "Why Accountability Is Vital to Your Company," Forbes, 6 Oct 2019, https://www.forbes.com/sites/johnhall/2019/10/06/why-accountability-is-vital-to-your-company/?sh=62daa1206580.

13 Erin Hutchinson, "Meaning through Mentorship: The Value of the Professional Role Model," Forbes, 15 Apr 2022, https://www.forbes.com/sites/forbescommunicationscouncil/2022/04/15/meaning-through-mentorship-the-value-of-the-professional-role-model/?sh=78212de45f57.

14 Ken Cook, "Patton's big leadership lesson (and how you can apply it today)," Cited in various sources, including The Business Journals, 8 July 2015, https://www.bizjournals.com/bizjournals/how-to/growth-strategies/2015/07/pattons-big-leadership-lesson.html.

15 Colin M. Fisher, Teresa M. Amabile, and Julianna Pillemer, "How to Help (Without Micromanaging)," HBR, Jan-Feb 2020, https://hbr.org/2021/01/how-to-help-without-micromanaging.

16 Ryan Holiday, The Obstacle Is the Way (New York: Penguin Books, 2014), 16.

17 Jacki Ross, "6 Reasons Employees Aren't Taking Professional Development," Skillswave, https://www.d2l.com/blog/2021/11/30/reasons-employees-arent-using-professional-development/.

18 Ross.

19 Ted Godbout, "Without Development Opportunities, Most Professionals Likely to Leave," NAPA, 12 July 2022, https://www.napa-net.org/news-info/daily-news/without-development-opportunities-most-professionals-likely-leave.

20 Ilene S. Cohen, Ph.D., "The Lifelong Journey of Personal Development," *Psychology Today*, 13 Dec 2023, https://www.psychologytoday.com/intl/blog/your-emotional-meter/202312/the-lifelong-journey-of-personal-development.

21 Patrick Lencioni, "Make Your Values Mean Something," *Harvard Business Review*, July 2002, https://hbr.org/2002/07/make-your-values-mean-something.

22 "Just a Little Bit More," Cited by many sources, including *Breakpoint Colson Center*, 10 Apr 1999, https://breakpoint.org/just-little-bit/.

23 Cited in Arthur C. Brooks, *From Strength to Strength* (New York, NY: Portfolio Penguin, 2022) 59.

24 "Why & How Your Employees are Wasting Time at Work" *Salary.com*, https://www.salary.com/articles/why-how-your-employees-are-wasting-time-at-work/.

25 Thomas Simon, "Time Waster Activities at Work," *Monitask Blog*, https://www.monitask.com/en/blog/time-wasting-work.

26 Ron Carucci, "4 Ways Lying Becomes the Norm at a Company," *Harvard Business Review*, 15 Feb 2019, https://hbr.org/2019/02/4-ways-lying-becomes-the-norm-at-a-company.

27 Carucci.

28 Seth Godin, "Define: Brand," *Seth's Blog*, 13 December, https://seths.blog/2009/12/define-brand/.

29   Cited in Eric Savitz, *"Listening to Social Media Doesn't Mean Ceding Control,"* Patrick Salyer, Updated 17 Aug 2012, *Forbes*, https://www.forbes.com/sites/ciocentral/2012/08/04/listening-to-social-media-cues-doesnt-mean-ceding-control/?sh=61f79f91cd52.

30   Carol Roth, "3 Examples of When Being Cheap Is Costly for Your Business,", *Entrepreneur*, 23 Aug 2016, https://www.entrepreneur.com/living/3-examples-of-when-being-cheap-is-costly-for-your-business/281195.

31   Jon Staff, "Starting a Business Is Not as Risky as You Think: Don't Be Afraid to Take the Plunge," *Inc.*, 4 Aug 2022, https://www.inc.com/jon-staff/starting-a-business-is-not-as-risky-as-you-think.html.

32   Jeremy Ames, "6 Ways Businesses Can Fail from the Beginning," *Inc.*, 3 May 2024, https://www.inc.com/entrepreneurs-organization/6-ways-businesses-can-fail-from-beginning.html.

33   Robin Abrahams and Boris Groysberg, "How to Become a Better Listener," *Harvard Business Review*, 21 Dec 2021, https://hbr.org/2021/12/how-to-become-a-better-listener.

34   Abrahams and Groysberg, "How to Become a Better Listener."

35   C. S. Lewis, *Mere Christianity* (San Francisco, CA: Harper, February 6, 2001) 135.

36   David Foster Wallace, "This Is Water," Kenyon College commencement address, 2005, https://fs.blog/david-foster-wallace-this-is-water/.

37   Dr. Margie Warrell, "Pursue a Cause Greater than Yourself: The Heart of True Leadership," *Forbes*, 8 Dec 2018, https://www.forbes.com/sites/margiewarrell/2018/12/08/why-doing-good-is-ultimate-success-strategy/?sh=64d2e2316478.

www.ingramcontent.com/pod-product-compliance
Lightning Source LLC
Chambersburg PA
CBHW050906160426
43194CB00011B/2308